To John,
with
everlasting
Love
X

DESIGN MASTERCLASS
KELLY HOPPEN MBE

jacqui small

HOW TO ACHIEVE THE HOME OF YOUR DREAMS

TEXT BY HELEN CHISLETT

PHOTOGRAPHS BY MEL YATES

Foreword by Savannah Miller, Sienna Miller and Natasha Corrett 6
Introduction 8

THE GROUNDWORK 12
Function 14
The Space 20
Natural Light 24
Architectural Features 26
Planning Your Space 36
The Zones 41
The Flow 42
The Grid 44
The Design Brief 54
Plans and Planning 56
Reading Plans 56
Understanding Scale 56
Drawing Up a Floor Plan 57
Elevations 58
Perspectives 58
CGI (Computer-Generated Image) 58

DESIGN CONSIDERATIONS 60
The Bones of Good Design 62
Symmetry and Balance 66
Scale and Proportion 70
Creating Impact 74
The Art of Juxtaposition 78
Lighting Design 80
How to Design a Lighting Scheme 82
The Whole Effect 94
Wall and Floor Finishes 96
Walls 98
Floors 100
Colour, Texture and Pattern 102
Colour Palettes 104
Texture 123
Cabinetry 132
Doors 136
Furniture 138
Furniture Layout 144
Soft Furnishings 148
Window Treatments 152
Upholstery 158
Cushions 159
Runners and Throws 159
Accessories 162
The Art of Display 164
Mood Enhancement 172

DESIGNING ROOMS 174
Creating a Good Impression: The Core of the Home 176
The Front Door 176
Entrance Halls 178
Stairs 180
Circulation and Flow 182
Lighting 184
Gather Together: Living Rooms 186
Key Considerations 188
Layout 190
Style 192
Lighting 194
Display 196
Home Studies 200
Cook and Chat: Kitchens 202
Style 202
Key Considerations 205
Layout 205
Functionality 206
Lighting 210
Decoration and Detailing 212
A Sense of Occasion: Dining Rooms 214
Key Considerations 216
Furniture 218
Style 220
Lighting 222
Accessories 224
Private Moments: Bedrooms 226
Key Considerations 228
Furniture 232
Style 232
Lighting 236
Dressing Rooms 238
Children's Rooms 240
Special Sanctuary: Bathrooms 244
Key Considerations 246
Style 248
Layout 250
Lighting 252
Decoration and Detailing 254
Guest Cloakrooms 256
Downtime: Exercise and Leisure Rooms 258
Pools and Spas 260
Gyms 262
Media Rooms 263

PROJECT MANAGEMENT 264
The Basics 264
The Schedule 264
Managing the Budget 265
Assembling and Managing the Team 267
Living on Site 268
Snagging 268
Involving an Architect 268

Address Book 270
Acknowledgements and Credits 271

Page 1 A collection of mirrors with deep metal frames creates an installation on the wall of this living room.

Page 2 A rich, gold specialist plaster finish plays against the oak joinery of a custom-made door and the wrought-iron staircase beyond.

Opposite Gold-leafed mirrors reflect the metallic sheen of the dining-room pendant lights.

First published in 2013 by
Jacqui Small LLP
An imprint of Aurum Press Ltd
74–77 White Lion Street
London N1 9PF

Text copyright © Kelly Hoppen 2013

Photography, design and layout copyright © Jacqui Small 2013

The author's moral rights have been asserted.

All rights reserved. No part of this book may be reproduced, stored in a retrieval system, or transmitted, in any form or by any means, electronic, electrostatic, magnetic tape, mechanical, photocopying, recording or otherwise, without prior permission in writing from the publisher.

A catalogue record for this book is available from the British Library.

PUBLISHER Jacqui Small
MANAGING EDITOR Lydia Halliday
ART DIRECTOR Lawrence Morton
PROJECT EDITOR Zia Mattocks
PRODUCTION Peter Colley

ISBN 978 1 909342 02 6

2021
10

Printed and bound in China

Every effort has been made to trace copyright holders of artworks and designs. We apologize in advance for any unintentional omissions and would be pleased to insert the appropriate acknowledgement in any subsequent publication.

FOREWORD

What does home mean to you?

Home is a place where you feel safe, an environment in which you can be utterly yourself. It is, most certainly, more than just a space to rest one's head. Home is a manifestation of your life, whoever you are and whatever that means to you. We suppose that is why, as sisters, when we spend time in each other's homes, we feel, in some respect, that we are in a home away from home. There is a familiarity in the energy of the interior that cannot be denied.

Having been brought up together – our lives entwined at least half of the time, anyway – we have all ended up with homes that have a common thread in their design. We put that down to our homes reflecting who we are as people. Although we all believe there is definitely some weight in the old adage that a tidy home means a tidy head, much to Kelly's dismay, not one of us has ever fully got to grips with that.

If you can take one thing from *Design Masterclass*, let it be this: Kelly understands the geography and energy of interiors like no one else. If you take style tips from her and keep your own personality in everything you do, your home will flow, be beautiful, and be a true reflection of you and your family. Your home is an extension of yourself, and you should never feel uncomfortable and out of place in your own environment. Rather, it should be a place where you can grow and thrive, and become the best person you can be and the person you have always wanted to be. Kelly really knows how to make the very best of every home she works on – and every situation she is in, for that matter. She has a unique ability to understand people – their nature, their shortcomings – and so the way she designs can genuinely enhance your quality of life.

We know this because we have experienced it first-hand. And we are all so proud to call her Mum, in some capacity. She has been and always will be, in some way, 'home' to us.

With all our love,
Savannah, Sienna and Natasha

Opposite An unusual view of a bespoke wrought-iron and oak staircase reflected in a pair of convex mirrors.

INTRODUCTION

Creating a beautiful home for you and your family is one of the greatest pleasures in life. The whole experience of 'coming home' is one we value more and more in a world that is fast, noisy and, at times, threatening. The moment we cross our threshold, we feel the cares slip from our shoulders and we are cocooned in comfort, safety and warmth. Our homes are our greatest asset, not just financially but also for our sense of well-being and happiness.

Design Masterclass is about helping you design and decorate your own home and, in so doing, achieve that sense of calm and relaxation. When I began my design school in 2001, it was driven by the need to give something back. I started my business at the age of 16 and a half, and I feel incredibly fortunate not only to have survived three economic recessions, but also to have seen my own vision for interior design embraced and accepted by so many people around the world. I am privileged that the 'Kelly Hoppen look' is one that is widely recognized – and has become a phrase synonymous with neutral palettes, beautiful textures and an East-meets-West aesthetic. However, I am an intuitive designer, rarely analysing why something works and something else does not. When I founded the design school, it forced me to really think about what I do and find a way of guiding students through the process from two-dimensional concept to three-dimensional reality. I see this book – and my previous design books – as my legacy, a way of putting down on paper everything that I carry in my head.

When I began the school, what surprised me most was how unconfident students were when faced with putting together design boards to show the combinations of floor materials, wall textures, furniture shapes and fabrics they had chosen. However, it is the sheer scale of what is on offer today

that people find so confusing. I often say that when designing a room, you should try to use the analogy of how you get dressed. The clothes, shoes and accessories that you choose for a night out, as opposed to a walk in the country, are entirely suited to the occasion and location. Your home is not so very different. I always begin a fabric scheme with linen, because it is the ideal foundation for other textures and colours and is what the Kelly Hoppen look is all about. It is the equivalent of a great pair of blue jeans that you can either dress up or dress down. Similarly, when you finish a room, you need to add the 'jewellery' – the accessories, flowers and art that really bring it alive. Neutrals are the equivalent of the 'little black dress' – the classic staple that never dates and that can be worn in so many different ways – and texture is everything.

Once you begin to understand the parallels between dressing yourself and dressing your home, it makes it much easier to focus on making the right choices. Rather than becoming distracted and confused by the myriad possibilities, you can train your eye to pick out those textures and materials that work for you – just as you would when shopping for clothes. Exercise your imagination and become a visual master. Be cautious, however. It is easy to get carried away by something gaudy and glitzy, but it may be the equivalent of the party dress you have never dared to actually wear. In order for your home to feel welcoming and comfortable, it must 'fit' you in the same way that a made-to-measure Savile Row suit does.

Design Masterclass is a consolidation of everything I taught at the school (time commitments mean that I can no longer run it myself). It is my way of holding your hand through the journey of designing a home, from analysing the space you have and determining how best to use it, to resolving choices of flooring, fabrics, furniture and lighting. In many ways, I have approached it as though the reader were a semi-professional. There seems little point in talking about furniture layouts, for example, unless you can understand how to use floor plans and scaled cut-outs. It also seems to me essential that you know how to project-manage well, because creating a home also means running budgets, managing building teams and implementing schedules. When I design a home for a client, my studio produces computer-generated images (CGIs) of what each room will look like – what is astounding is that, in the end, you can struggle to tell the difference between the CGI and a photograph of the real, finished room. My hope is that by following the advice in *Design Masterclass* you will have the same sensation of having created exactly the effect you intended from the start.

However, there is another layer to this book. It is not simply a blueprint of how to interior-design a home, but a specific guide to achieving the Kelly Hoppen look. While I am hugely flattered by the number of people who want to do just that, I can't help but notice that so often they do not get it right. It may sound obsessional, but the way that cushions are arranged, the height a picture is hung, or the angle at which a chair is placed really can make all the difference – there is a knack to it, which I hope will become clearer if you study the images on the following pages. There are also three words that you will find repeated throughout the book: zone, grid and flow. Believe me, if you can master these three concepts, you are very nearly there.

The interiors shown in *Design Masterclass* are a selection of projects that I have undertaken around the world over the past few years. I am hugely grateful to my various clients for allowing me to share their beautiful homes with you. I sincerely hope that this book will give you the tools and the insight to achieve your own version of a Kelly Hoppen interior, should you so desire. But more than that, I hope you design a home that is all about You.

THE GROUNDWORK

FUNCTION

The design process is focused on two essential factors: function and space. These are at the root of great design, so don't consider this the 'boring' stage – it is anything but. Understanding these two all-important aspects will help you to determine every decorating choice you make, from where to place the sofa to what colour to paint the walls.

It is people who determine function. Who lives in this house? Partner? Children? Animals? Your challenge is to come up with a design that will keep everyone happy, content that their own activities have been recognized and well catered for. There is no point in designing and decorating what you consider to be the perfect home, if it becomes a source of family discord. Compromise is a valuable tool. Give everyone something and peace will reign.

Write a wish list for your home. Don't worry about colour palettes, fabric choices or furniture layouts at this stage. Describe the atmosphere you want to achieve, the style of decoration you like, the things that will make you most happy, and how you want others to feel when they walk through the door.

The first thing to consider is what everyone who lives here likes to do. Which activities are carried out? First, list the obvious ones: work, rest, cook, entertain, bathe, sleep, play and so on. Then add the more personal ones: hobbies, games, fitness and so forth. Ask each member of the family to write down what they most want from the 'new' house. They might not be able to have everything they want, but perhaps you can make sure that everyone gets something.

Unless you have an enormous house, the chances are that rooms will have to double up for certain functions. A dining room might also be a part-time home office, a bedroom might also be a yoga space, and a conservatory could be a play area. When assessing each room, think carefully about how many activities take place in it, who uses it and when. The secret of multi-functionality is in the way a space is zoned (see page 41).

The function of a room affects every aspect of how it is designed and decorated, but in particular it has a direct impact on lighting. Every activity that is carried out in a room needs to be lit appropriately, whether with bright task lighting (when chopping vegetables, for instance) or gentle mood lighting (when relaxing through yoga or Pilates, perhaps). So you not only have to decide *what* will happen in a particular room, but *where* exactly within that room. Functionality is at the root of a successful lighting scheme (see also pages 80–95).

Function also determines how much storage you will need and where it is best situated. Children's toys, for example, are often bulky and bright – you might want to tuck them out of sight in the evening when you reclaim your living space. Family snugs full of DVDs and games need a storage solution that is both tidy and logical. Bathrooms need storage solutions both for small-scale items, such as cotton buds, and large-scale ones, such as home-spa equipment. Whether storage is built-in or freestanding is an important part of the decorating scheme and will affect aspects of budget and scheduling.

ANALYSING YOUR NEEDS

- What sort of life do you envisage leading in this house?
- How can the space be made to 'work' for you?
- Who lives here with you?
- What do they like/need to do?
- Where do these activities usually take place?
- How much space do they require for these activities?
- At what time of day and with what frequency?
- Can rooms be designed to double up in terms of functionality through zoning?
- How will zones affect questions of lighting and storage within the room?

This page Think function first, particularly in a bathroom where unsightly plumbing and electrics must be concealed. A freestanding tap unit, in the same stone as the runner on the floor and wall, conceals lighting and other essentials.

Previous spread In a family house that is also a welcoming sociable hub, the kitchen-cum-dining room is the heartbeat of the home. The white leather stools along the breakfast bar of the Boffi kitchen are ideal for both children and adults who may want to 'graze' at different times. They balance perfectly with classic Wishbone dining chairs by Hans Wegner, used mainly in the evening or for more formal occasions. Different scales of ceiling pendant lights accentuate the two zones.

Above Whatever the room, the position of the television will play a central part in determining the furniture layout, but it should not intrude when not in use. The media wall in this living space has pull-out storage units with leather runners that provide ample space for DVDs, computer games and the like.

Right At the other end of the same room as on the previous spread, an L-shaped seating configuration connects the living space to the kitchen, making conversation between the two easy, while also allowing for comfortable downtime in front of the television. A pair of ebonized hand-carved tables marks out the invisible boundary between the zones, while also echoing the installation of deep-framed mirrors on the wall behind.

THE SPACE

Having considered what you and your family need from your home, you now have to find ways of making the space you have fulfil those needs. The success of interior design is dependent on a lot more than the decorative ingredients.

First, you have to get to know your house. Walk around it and take a long, hard look at the rooms and how they relate and link to each other. Which ones work as they are, in terms of dimensions, proportions and natural light, and which don't? Consider whether it is possible to knock through walls and reconfigure an existing space (structural constraints permitting). Perhaps a tiny bedroom would be better as a bathroom, or a dining room as a family snug? Take advice from architects or structural engineers where appropriate (see page 268) and keep your options open.

Think about flow, too – the way that people walk around the house and what they see as they go. Just as a garden designer creates a landscape that shows off the views to full advantage, so you need to be aware of the internal vistas within your home. Stand in key rooms and look through to adjoining ones – how can you place furniture, artwork and decorative objects to create the greatest impact? Perhaps you could make simple improvements, such as replacing a standard single door with two double-height ones, or moving a radiator to a less obtrusive spot.

Be sympathetic to the architecture. You don't have to produce a pastiche of the original style or period, but you should allow the internal bones of your home to lead certain decisions. Just as you choose clothes to suit your own figure, so you should opt for decorating schemes that best complement the house you have chosen. There is no reason why you cannot marry contemporary design with period architecture, but the trick is in retaining attractive internal features, such as fireplaces and original coving, rather than pretending the property is something it is not (see Architectural Features, page 26). Acknowledge the past while living in the present.

Where your house is situated will also have an impact. A city house surrounded by brick and concrete feels very different internally to one that is in the midst of green countryside. It is not just a question of light – although light is undoubtedly a factor – it is also to do with the colours and textures that are reflected into the home. Where a property is sited will also affect whether you want to block out unattractive views or embrace fabulous ones. If your house is surrounded by garden, you may want to re-landscape it to reflect the internal design philosophy.

Any structural changes or inherent problems, such as damp or timber decay, have to be tackled well in advance of trying to bring your design vision to fruition. Be honest about any expensive and time-consuming improvements that need to be made to plumbing, wiring, insulation, home security, audio-visual (AV) systems and such like. There is no point trying to shortcut any of this; your new home must function effectively at every practical level. Seek professional advice and build these costs, with a generous contingency fund of at least 20 per cent, into your budget from the beginning.

Opposite The art of designing a large living area is to make sure that different zones are clearly demarcated and that there is a comfortable flow between each one. Here there are three main seating areas, connected visually by the grid of contrasting wood running along each side of a central runner of lacquered timber. The line of vision is broken neatly by the sculptural floating shelf made of silver-lacquered resin, 'Dune 01' (2007) by Zaha Hadid (Editions David Gill, London), and the line of tall cylindrical glass vases.

Overleaf A bird's-eye view in a double-height apartment from the top of the spiral staircase that leads to the entrance hall. The height of the windows is echoed in the vertical lines of the custom-made bookcases on each side of the fireplace. The pale taupe timber floor sets the tone for the rest of the monochromatic scheme – charcoal, black and accents of yellow and bronze.

ASSESSING SPACE

- → How does light travel around the house by day?
- → Does the property benefit from views that you wish to maximize?
- → What is the style of architecture – both internal and external?
- → What are your home's key qualities?
- → What are its bad points?
- → Can the above be solved by a new configuration of space?
- → What structural problems need to be tackled and solved?
- → Would it help to consult with professionals, such as an architect or a structural engineer?
- → How does the space flow from room to room?
- → How can you make the most of internal vistas?
- → What is the impression you have of the house when you stand outside and look at it?
- → How can you best link the outside with the inside?
- → Why did you fall in love with the house in the first place?

ASSESSING NATURAL LIGHT

- → Take time to study changes of light during the day and over the seasons.
- → Don't fight with light – allow it to lead you to certain decorating solutions.
- → Observe which rooms are 'morning' and which 'evening'; then decide which are 'winter' and which 'summer'.
- → Decide whether you need to artificially boost the natural daylight in any rooms, perhaps through the use of uplighters.
- → Consider whether you can use reflective surfaces to enhance the natural light and magnify its effect.

Every house has its awkward spaces – dark corners, difficult proportions or odd shapes. The trick is to draw attention to those areas that have more light, harmony or symmetry, so making the tricky places less visible. If a room is lacking in symmetry, perhaps with an off-centre fireplace, don't make that fireplace too much of a focal point. Instead, introduce another 'Wow!' factor into the scheme, such as a magnificent piece of furniture or a striking painting, and let the eye be drawn to that. In rooms that are unusual shapes, don't try to impose a symmetry that is not there, but look for ways of restoring balance to the design, perhaps by hanging a group of paintings on one wall, or positioning furniture in such a way that it creates a cosy and comfortable effect. With thought, you can imprint a feeling of order and harmony onto a room that might naturally have little of either.

There will be plenty of moments along the design journey where you lose sight of what you originally loved about your property, especially when you are surrounded by builder's dust and rubble. So, this is a good moment to write down the features and qualities that first attracted you to your home, which will guide you when making various and detailed design decisions. Acknowledging the good points should help you to create a design that embraces and emphasizes them.

Natural Light

Daylight is one of the most important ingredients in a home. If you are lucky enough to have big rooms that are flooded with light, embrace that fact and forget about hanging heavy curtains or chunky blinds. Don't despair if you have some north-facing rooms that appear dark and dingy even in the middle of a summer's afternoon. Accept that they are evening rooms and decorate and use them accordingly. One of the worst things you can do is to paint a dull room brilliant white; it will only look murky and grey. It is better to paint a dark room in a rich, moody shade and embrace its nocturnal character.

If it is practical to do so, live in the house for a few months before making decisions about design and decoration. Studying the movement of light at different times of the day and year gives you the chance to see how it is affected by external factors, such as buildings or trees. What you learn from the way light travels can influence your decision regarding the function of the rooms. You may decide to locate key rooms, such as the kitchen or family room, in places that benefit from good levels of daylight, for instance. It will also indicate whether natural light needs to be artificially boosted in some way – particularly in the winter – and whether you need window treatments that allow more light into a room or enable you to filter it out at certain times.

Below In the city, there is a balance to be had between encouraging natural light into the home and still maintaining privacy from adjacent buildings. Shutters are the ideal way of achieving this, while also creating interesting effects of light and shadow. Reflective surfaces, such as glass and metal, maximize the feeling of light by bouncing it back into the room, as do any glossy surfaces, including gloss paint and metallic fabrics.

ARCHITECTURAL FEATURES

The architectural features of a room are its core structure. If you own a period home, you may have inherited a wealth of beautiful and interesting fireplaces, dados, cornicing and such like. If so, you should leave well alone – they might be protected by law anyway. Even very contemporary decoration schemes can look fantastic against this backdrop. Not all period features are attractive, however, and many of those added later in a house's history will be at odds with the architectural style and detract from the success of a room. Consider carefully what should stay and what should go. Scale is also a factor, particularly in the case of doors and skirting boards, which often look mean in relation to the height of a room.

Fireplaces

If a fireplace is authentic to the house, then the general rule is to leave it alone. Fireplaces are natural focal points within a room, particularly if you are lucky enough to have one that can be used. Mantelpieces also provide an obvious display area. However, if a fireplace is a later addition – and not harmonious with the architectural style – then you should feel no guilt in ripping it out.

This page and opposite
Contemporary fireplaces come in many sizes, materials and shapes, including this double-aspect variety, which can be enjoyed here from both the hall and the living room (see page 187). Protected by glass, it is safe as well as visually striking. The low, rectangular design emphasizes the grid structure inherent in both rooms (see page 44).

Radiators

If you are decorating a house from scratch, you have the advantage of being able to position radiators exactly where you require them, or to install underfloor heating if appropriate. If you have inherited someone else's heating system, don't assume you must keep either the radiator style or the position. There is definitely a case for moving a radiator if it is taking up a wall where you would like to locate a piece of furniture or display a great work of art. However, any plumbing alteration has cost implications, so you must weigh the practical and financial disadvantages against the stylistic advantages.

Staircases

The staircase is the pivot around which a home rotates. It is not just a transition area between one level and another; it can be an extraordinary piece of architectural sculpture that lifts a property to a new dimension of design. While not everyone can afford to have a staircase custom-made, as those shown here, it is often possible to improve an existing one by changing the banisters, rethinking the lighting, upgrading the flooring and, of course, by completely redecorating. Even something as simple as changing a dowdy stair carpet to one that has been elegantly bordered can make all the difference to a staircase's visual impact.

Below A bird's-eye view down the central well of a custom-built oak and wrought-iron staircase. The specially commissioned lights by Kevin Reilly have a dark patina frame with clear glass shades, and are suspended at different levels.

Opposite The same staircase, but this time of the basement view, with the lights reflected in the glass top of a circular table.

This page The first floor of the spectacular staircase shown on the previous pages, illustrating the grandeur of the custom-made wrought-iron banisters and the oak treads and floor. The Kevin Reilly pendant lights punctuate the different levels.

Opposite A series of backlit slatted timber archways increase the sense of drama in this impressive entrance hallway and draw the eye along it to the reception area at the end.

Above and opposite These bespoke double-height doors have been designed as functional sculpture, with vertical and horizontal figurations of stained oak hand-picked for each panel. Their scale, geometry and tactility combine to make them a key feature within the interior of this magnificent home. Grid-like door furniture is elegant but unobtrusive, keeping attention focused on the doors themselves. The varnished oak floor is the ideal foundation for this 'installation' of internal joinery.

Windows

Modern windows detract from the beauty of historic architecture, so it is better to repair the original ones than to replace them. If cold is an issue, you could consider installing secondary glazing, which is less permanent and obtrusive than double glazing, or hang very thick interlined curtains or blinds.

Doors

Being the most dominant feature of joinery, doors need due consideration. Generally speaking, it is better to scale them up so that they become a statement, rather than trying to camouflage them into the walls. However, you also have to be aware that they can look monolithic if unadorned in any way. Doors provide another surface on which to introduce an additional layer of texture into the room and it is fun to introduce a mix to the design – wood with cane, leather, fabric or vellum, perhaps. Handles, too, are as central to the impact of the design as the timber you choose.

Built-in Cabinetry

You might regret removing existing cabinetry, because it is very expensive to install from scratch. If you don't like the style, think about whether it is possible to replace the doors and add your own choice of statement door handle. Storage is such an essential ingredient of a room that the more there is, the better.

Power Points and Switches

In order to know where power points should be located, you will first have to think out a basic furniture layout (see page 144). This, in turn, will guide you as to where electronic equipment, such as AV systems, may be positioned and where lamps will be needed. Think, too, about where light switches should be placed. Fit dimmers wherever possible, because the more control you have with lighting, the better the results will be. Floor sockets can be a useful addition, but be careful – once a floor is cut into, whether it be a hard material, such as stone, or a soft one, such as carpet, there is no going back.

Cornicing, Dados and Ceiling Roses

Original cornicing should be left alone, but do not be tempted to add a faux style to a contemporary home, as it will always look wrong. Dados and picture rails can be attractive in the right setting, but if their original use – to make a divide between two wall coverings or to hang paintings – has been lost, then you could consider removing them and freeing up wall space accordingly.

Skirting Boards

Generally speaking, the deeper the skirting board, the better. Choose a style that is appropriate to the age and architectural style of your home. Skirtings should be painted the same shade as the walls: do not make them a feature by painting them a contrasting colour.

Opposite A sculpted staircase of wood and glass seen in the smoky glass of the media wall of the adjacent living room. The way the light catches the glass adds a layer of additional beauty. A deep lava-stone shelf runs the full length of this room, stepping down under the television, providing a display area for candles and other objects.

Below In the lobby of an apartment building in Moscow, a black marbled stone has been chosen for the walls, echoing the rich tones of black timber on the floors. The artwork is from the Kelly Hoppen range.

PLANNING YOUR SPACE

This page and previous spread In any room, but particularly one as large as this, it is important to plan on paper where specific pieces of furniture are to go. Here the primary seating area has been marked out by four large white bronze floor lamps with silk shades by Robert Kuo, creating a central square within the space. The column of illuminated display niches is also a key feature, the pivot around which the rest of the room flows. Galion console tables by Christian Liaigre emphasize symmetry, while other pieces of furniture, such as the quilted linen day bed, are designed to provide visual punctuation.

Once you have finished the first assessment, both of the house and of how you want to live in it, it is time to get down to the real work of design. Don't rush to fill your space with fabrics, furniture and art. Successful interior design is all about taking care of every step along the way, ensuring that there is a natural logic between one decorating decision and the next. The first lesson is to 'see' space in a different way. You have to be able to envisage the grid, the zones and the flow (see below). These will form the basis of your design scheme.

The Zones

Most rooms have a level of multi-functionality within them. This means that you have to be aware of the zones within a room – what they are used for, who uses them and when. These zones define the layout of a room, affecting not only where you position the furniture, but also where to site lighting, power points, radiators and other essentials. The art is in achieving a room that looks seamless and unified, while also comprising different zones. You can do this by using the grid system (see pages 44–9) to subtly divide a space according to function. This may be through a change of flooring material, for example, or in the way a single piece of furniture is placed to screen one part of a room from another.

Large open-plan spaces lend themselves to zoning perfectly, but it can also be applied to smaller rooms. A bedroom might need an area for exercising on a mat, a place for dressing and a desk for correspondence. A kitchen is somewhere to cook and to eat, but may also be a place for children to do their homework, for the pet hamster to live and for displaying family photographs.

Zoning can also be about changing the mood when required. A bathroom may need to make you feel alert and refreshed in the morning, but relaxed and tranquil at night. A dining room may have to work as well for noisy family lunches as it does for more intimate supper parties.

Left Bold, sculptural pieces of lighting in bronze and LED tubes provide a key connection between the dining and living zones – very different (the near one by Sigma and the far one by Roll and Hill) but clearly related. The two areas are separated by floor-to-ceiling wooden slats, but can also be read as one uniform space in terms of materials, colours and forms. Note, for example, how the runners over the dining chairs are subtly echoed in the upholstery of the ottomans in front of the fireplace. A runner of stone in the timber floor marks out an invisible 'corridor' that connects this space with the adjacent ones.

The Flow

How people move through a space is crucial. It is important in terms of practicality – can you walk comfortably around a dining table once people are seated at it, or open a door without knocking into a piece of furniture? Floor plans are an important tool, therefore, when planning flow. However, there are also the less tangible issues of harmony, balance and mood to consider. If a space flows well, the room is more pleasant to be in. Flow is not only about how you physically move around, but also about what you see and experience as you go. It is not focused so much on the objects you have in a room, but the space around those objects; it is this that allows a house to breathe.

Flow needs to be considered in the property as a whole. It is important to have a sense of harmony as you walk from one room to the next, so that the eye and spirit are not jarred by sudden changes of tempo. Think about the views between adjacent rooms and how to capitalize on their impact. This doesn't mean decorating every room to be the same, but it does mean thinking about not only how a certain room might look, but also how it relates to the house as a whole.

Above and right Custom-made louvred screens, in the same finish as the central runner, are used here to divide the living room from the dining area when required. By allowing light to filter in, they encourage the feeling of flow, a far better solution than room dividers that would block the view entirely. The day bed, with its base of high-gloss lacquered steel and white upholstery, is by Sé. It has been placed in such a way as to form a visual break between one room and the other. The floor lamp is a vintage find.

The Grid

A room is a three-dimensional cuboid made up of six surfaces: floor, ceiling and four walls. Imagine these as planes on which you can play with vertical and horizontal lines. Don't confuse these lines with actual stripes. The vertical may be the height of a floor lamp or the fall of a blind. The horizontal may be floating shelves or a runner of wood in a stone floor. The important thing is to begin to see a space in a different way – not as an empty shell, but as a pure canvas on which the vertical and the horizontal can be explored. This grid structure can be echoed in every element you bring into a room, either in obvious ways, such as runners down curtains or bands on cushions, or in more subtle ways, such as how objects are arranged on a shelf.

The grid is the bone structure of a room. It forms a firm foundation to the rest of the decorating scheme and is essential for getting the internal architecture right. If everything is chosen and placed with the grid in mind, no ingredient will jar or look wrong.

You can use the grid to improve proportions. If you wish to make a room appear bigger, you can do so both by emphasizing the horizontal lines – through deep skirtings, dados and picture rails – and by accentuating the vertical ones – with floor-to-ceiling curtains, tall cabinetry, slim mirrors and so forth.

Above left The grid is not a restriction; rather, it allows you to take better control of a space. Even in the contours of a yacht, a simple grid on the floors and walls can imprint a sense of structure. Here, a taupe timber floor has been inlaid with a strip of polished chrome. The wooden runners on the walls are offset with padded linen.

Above right The same across-and-up effect can be achieved by doorways framing a floor grid. Here, a stone runner on a dark-stained timber floor guides the eye down the corridors that link one space to the next.

Opposite Rather than introducing a runner to the wall in paint or plaster, a floating wooden vertical panel has been chosen to make an even more dramatic statement. This is also a functional device, as lighting can be concealed behind it. A taupe marble runner has been inset into the timber floor, in effect, switching the materials. This provides a frame for the dining furniture and the bronze-and-parchment pendant above. The photographs are from the Kelly Hoppen range.

46 | THE GROUNDWORK

This page and opposite These six pictures illustrate what a dynamic effect boldly contrasting grids on floors can create, with polished marble runners set into black timber flooring. Not only do they lead the eye forwards, in effect providing a visual signpost of how to navigate the space, but they also provide a framework against which furniture and other objects can be placed. Whether used in a multi-directional configuration or as single features, they are impactful and energetic. Lighting has been integrated into the grooves of the wooden slatted arches, accentuating the feeling of drama and highlighting the bronze metal detailing of the reception desk and elevators. The freehand plan on the right illustrates how the grid has been used to drive the design forwards and direct the visitor to the key meeting and seating areas.

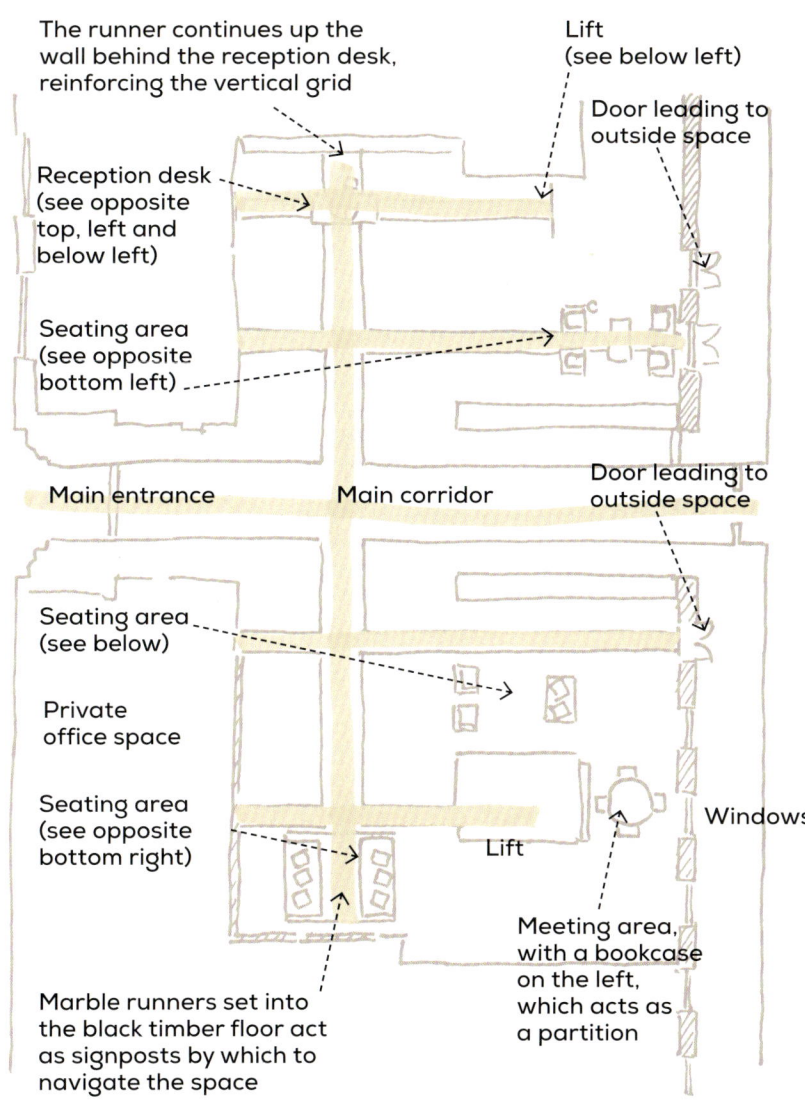

The runner continues up the wall behind the reception desk, reinforcing the vertical grid

Lift (see below left)

Reception desk (see opposite top, left and below left)

Door leading to outside space

Seating area (see opposite bottom left)

Main entrance

Main corridor

Door leading to outside space

Seating area (see below)

Private office space

Seating area (see opposite bottom right)

Lift

Windows

Meeting area, with a bookcase on the left, which acts as a partition

Marble runners set into the black timber floor act as signposts by which to navigate the space

PLANNING YOUR SPACE | 47

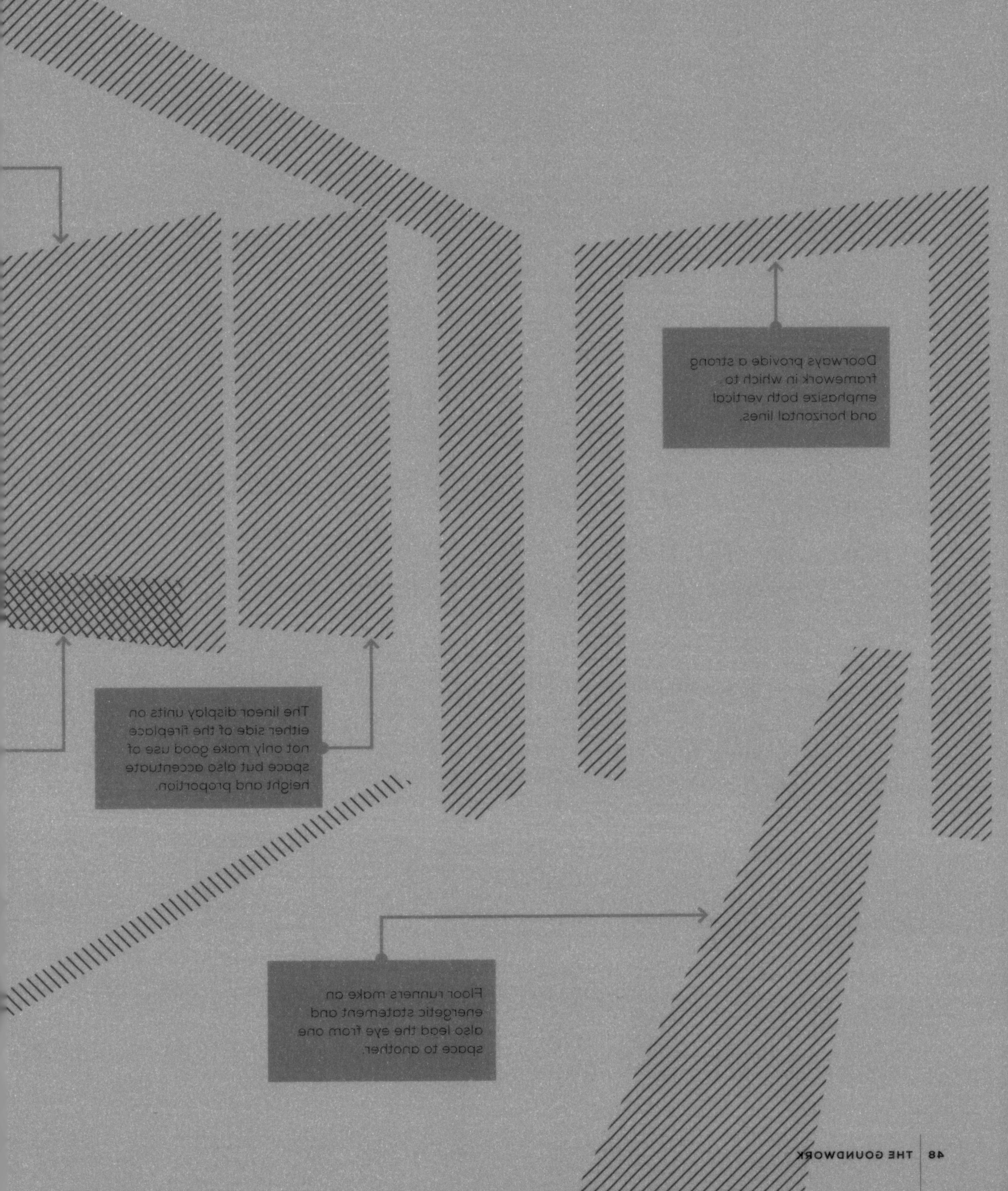

Doorways provide a strong framework in which to emphasize both vertical and horizontal lines.

The linear display units on either side of the fireplace not only make good use of space but also accentuate height and proportion.

Floor runners make an energetic statement and also lead the eye from one space to another.

The focal-point wall is a bold, rectangular block, inset with a television and fireplace, around which the seating is arranged.

Dark timber beams frame the view into the room, echoing the lines of the scaled-up doorways.

IN DETAIL **THE GRID**

The deconstruction of this monochromatic living area shows clearly how the horizontal and vertical planes have been harnessed to underpin the grid structure of the design. This applies not just to more obvious ingredients, such as the runner on the floor or the bold media wall, but also to the internal joinery, furniture and fireplace. These are the elements against which more organic pieces, such as the extraordinary light of bronze 'branches' and LED tubes, can play.

A low contemporary fireplace is the focal point of the horizontal planes of this interior.

The border of the carpet plays its part in the design's success, creating a frame upon the floor.

IN DETAIL **THE GRID**

The deconstruction of this monochromatic living area shows clearly how the horizontal and vertical planes have been harnessed to underpin the grid structure of the design. This applies not just to more obvious ingredients, such as the runner on the floor or the bold media wall, but also to the internal joinery, furniture and fireplace. These are the elements against which more organic pieces, such as the extraordinary light of bronze 'branches', and LED tubes, can play.

The focal-point wall is a bold, rectangular block, inset with a television and fireplace, around which the seating is arranged.

Dark timber beams frame the view into the room, echoing the lines of the scaled-up doorways.

A low contemporary fireplace is the focal point of the horizontal planes of this interior.

The border of the carpet plays its part in the design's success, creating a frame upon the floor.

IN DETAIL
SPACE PLANNING

00 This well-considered living, dining and kitchen area is a lesson in how to use all the space efficiently and effectively.

01 First, the room must be zoned according to function – here a sitting area and a kitchen-dining area occupy each end of a large open-plan space.

02 Zones can be subtly divided from one another by screens, as shown here, or by other pieces of furniture.

03 This then determines where the key pieces of furniture in each zone will go – in this case, the dining table and chairs, the generous seating and the coffee table.

04 Zoning also signposts where lights, power points, electrical cabling, light switches and other essentials are needed.

05 Make sure you have allowed enough space for the flow around the room and between pieces of furniture.

06 Be aware that the grid is made up of both vertical and horizontal lines, and consider how to emphasize these.

Left Developed as the Urban concept for Yoo, this scheme features taupe with red accents and a dark-stained timber floor, resulting in a crisp, monochromatic base that allows the eye to flow with ease from one area of the room to the other. The leather-upholstered furniture, hair-on-hide stool, cut-out screen, white-lacquered coffee table and trunk side tables are all from the Kelly Hoppen range. The large bronze-and-crystal light by Ochre provides an essential link between the adjacent living and dining zones, echoing the style and shape of the Ochre lights hung over the dining table.

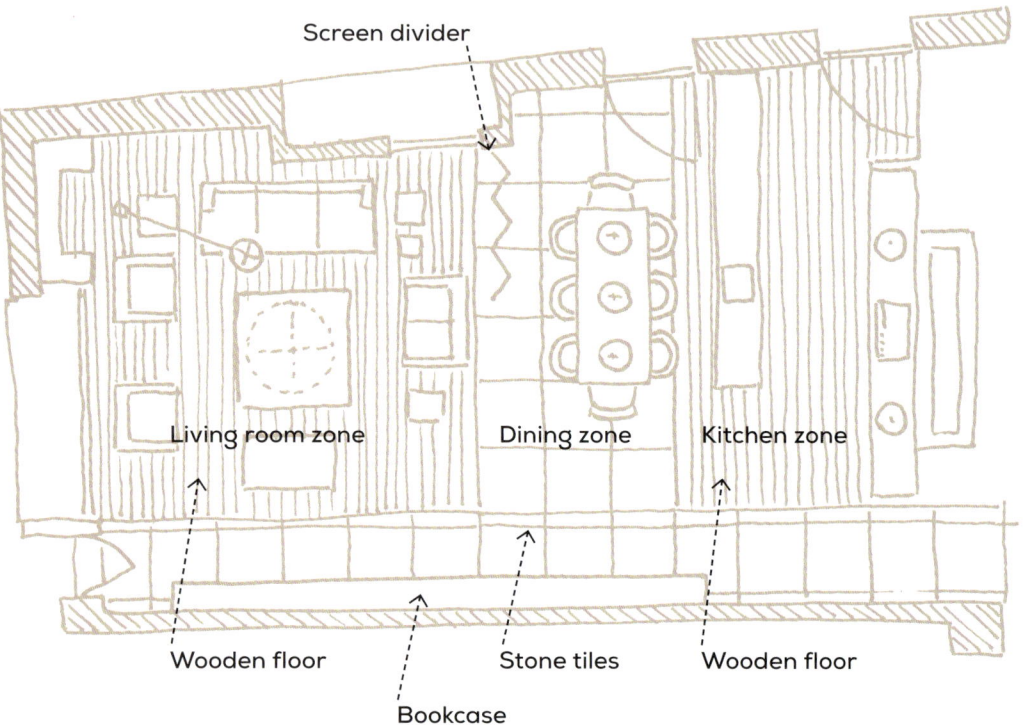

Screen divider

Living room zone   Dining zone   Kitchen zone

Wooden floor   Stone tiles   Wooden floor

Bookcase

Above and opposite The images on these pages show the same room from three different angles, illustrating the need to plan a space (see left) so that it can be enjoyed from every possible vista. The screen of cut-out panels is not designed to block the view so much as filter it, a subtle divide between the living and dining zones that allows the eye to pause, but does not entirely break the line of vision. The criss-cross shelving down one entire wall unites the two spaces, while also creating an energetic statement. The dining furniture is part of the Kelly Hoppen range.

Left The bird's-eye view offered by the plan shows how the central dining zone is the pivot between the living area on one side and the kitchen on the other.

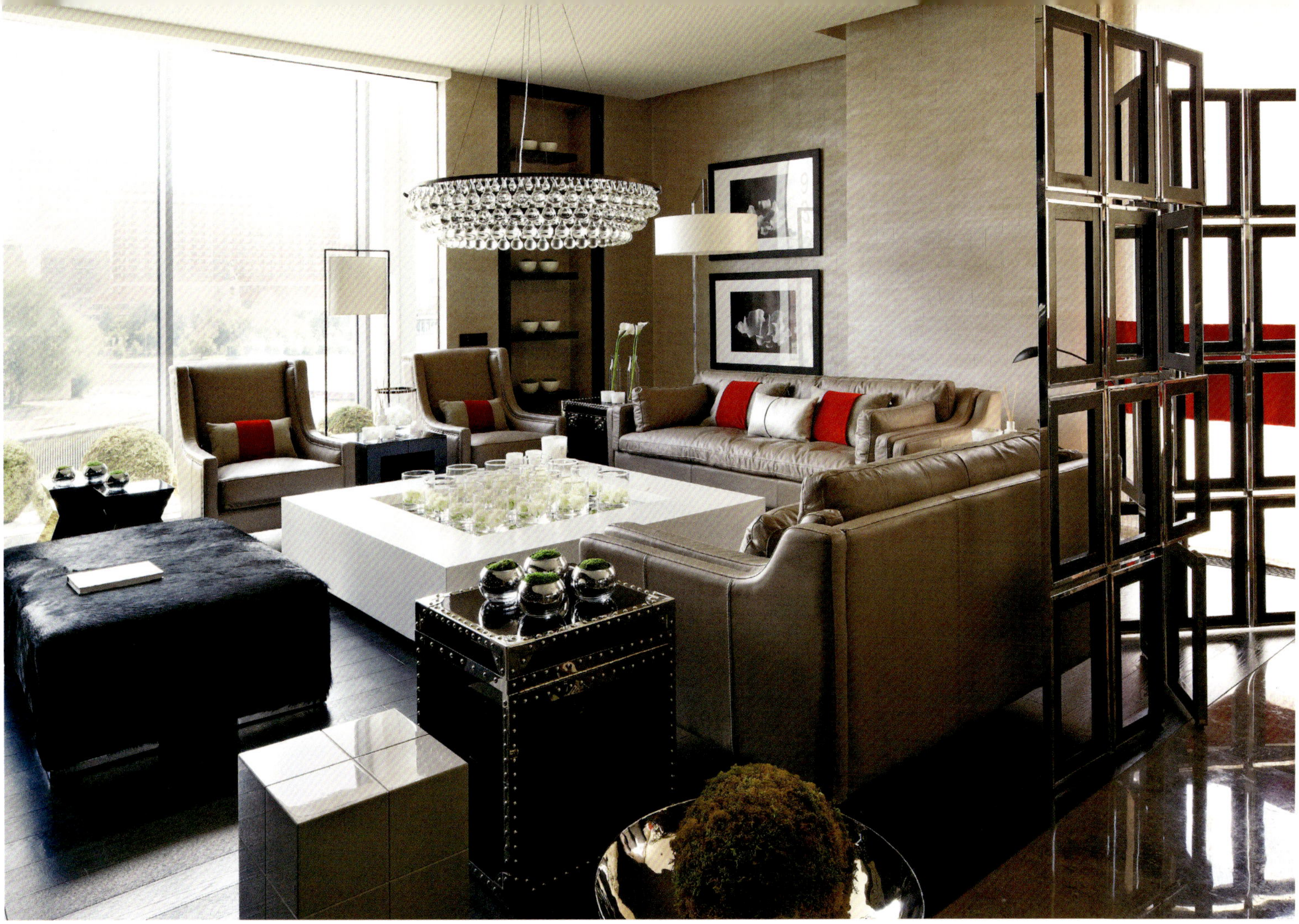

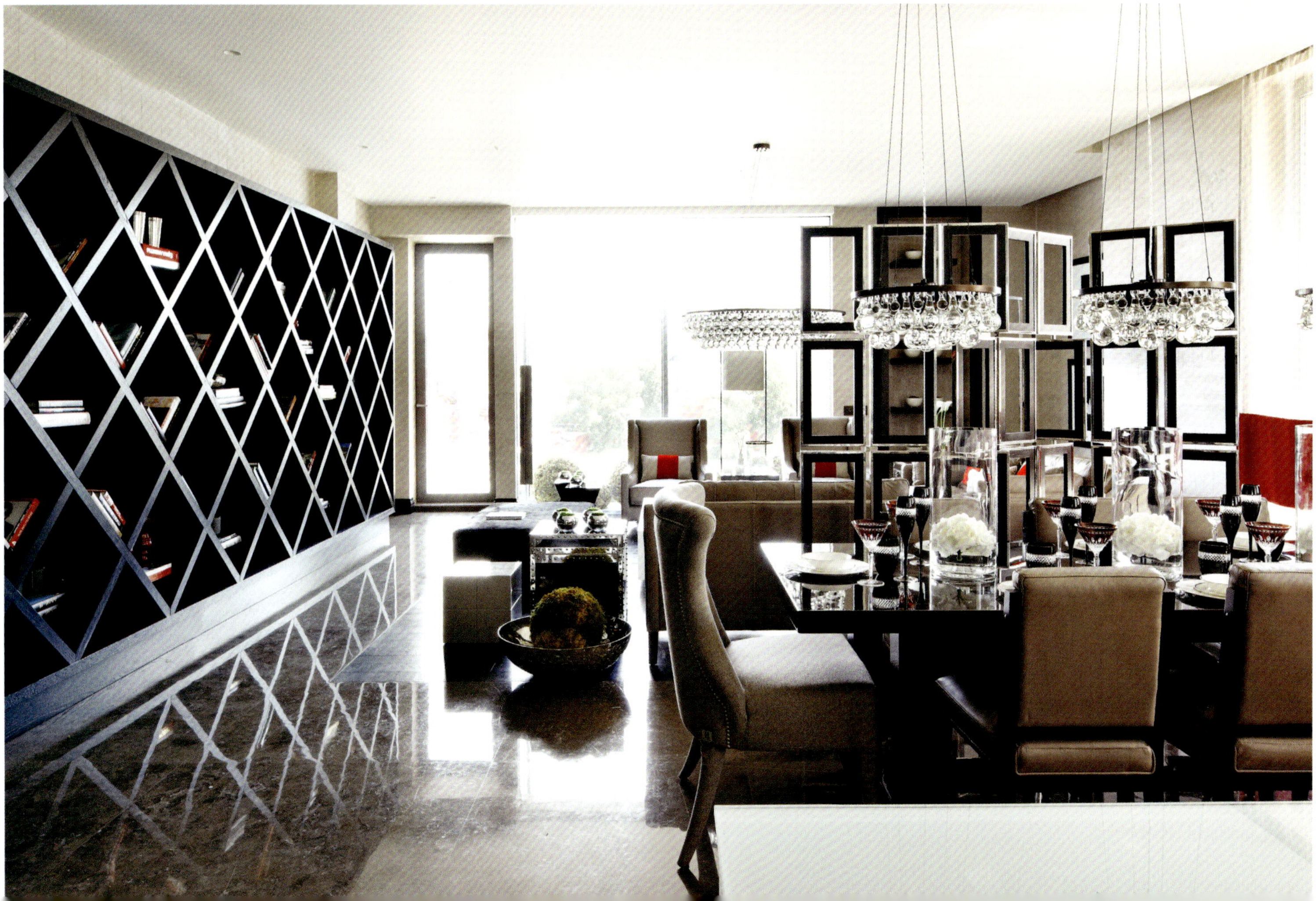

THE DESIGN BRIEF

Having asked numerous questions, thoroughly studied the good and bad points of the property, and listened to the needs of others who share the space, the next step is to write a design brief. The design brief is crucial to success, because without one it is so easy to become confused and to lose yourself in a maze of different decorating choices.

Tackle all the important points of the project: the people the design has to cater for; the style, age and location of the house; what you want from certain rooms; and the look you wish to create. Then begin to work out, step by step, how to achieve those aims. Think about which professionals you will need to draft in; how much money you can afford to allocate to each stage; how much time to allow; and so forth (see also Project Management, page 264).

Writing everything down will make you focus on the key areas of the home that need attention and it will be easier to prioritize effectively. It will also help to ensure that you don't lose confidence in your decisions while the property is being transformed. The brief is an important reminder of not only what you have decided to do, but also why you made those decisions in the first place. It is a way of staying in touch with your original dreams and vision.

Right For this art collector's home, full of fine paintings, sculpture, rare books and other treasured collections, the brief was to create a contemporary interior that was sympathetic to these possessions. Furniture has therefore been kept as 'silent' as possible, upholstered mainly in rich taupe linens and velvets. Vertical glass slats are fixed, but provide just enough separation between the sun room in the foreground and the living space beyond. A dark-stained timber floor and specialist plaster walls are a quiet foundation onto which the client's rare oriental rugs and works of art can be layered.

PLANS AND PLANNING

In order to plan your space effectively, you will need to understand floor plans and know how to measure up rooms accurately. It is easier to work out how to zone a space when looking at a paper plan than when you are standing in a room, because your eye will not be distracted by existing features. If a room is full of furniture, the temptation will be to replicate the same layout with alternative furniture and fittings. A plan encourages you to think afresh.

A floor plan is a way of conveying a variety of important information:

> The dimensions of the room.
> The shape of the room.
> The position of internal architectural features, such as doors, windows and fireplaces.
> How adjacent rooms connect to each other.

By making scaled versions of furniture and moving them around the plan (see opposite), you can determine the best layout. A plan will also tell you whether a piece of furniture will fit through the front door in the first place.

Reading Plans

Each plan contains a box in one corner – the legend box. This tells you:

> What you are looking at – one room, a series of rooms, or one area within a room.
> The scale.
> The paper size.
> The number, according to revisions made.
> Who made the latest revision.

The last two points matter, because everyone working on a project must be kept informed of any alterations to the brief. Numbering plans and asking the person who made the most recent changes to initial them is a way of communicating information to the whole team and will help to avoid disputes.

In order to read a plan accurately, you must print it on the correct size of paper (as itemized in the legend). If an architect or designer specifies A3 or A4 paper, for example, they have scaled the drawing to fit that paper size.

Design drawings, including floor plans, are produced to avoid ambiguities, so that you have redress if something goes wrong. That is why every version of every plan must be photocopied and distributed to every member of the building team, whether you think it relates to them or not.

Understanding Scale

When something is 1:1, it is a full-size replica of the given object. If it is 1:2, it is half the size of the given object. If it is 1:4, it is a quarter of the size – and so on. In other words, the smaller the second number, the greater the increase in scale (and the nearer it will be to the original dimensions).

Architects and designers use various scales according to the project, but the most usual is 1:100 (the room is shown at a hundredth of its size). To show more detail, they may increase the scale to 1:50 (the room is shown at a fiftieth of its size). Specialist contractors, such as joiners, may want to show even more detail and so produce drawings scaled 1:20.

You can ensure that furniture and other objects will fit the room by making paper cut-outs scaled to the correct size and moving these around the floor plan. The best way to do this is by using a scale ruler, which shows different scales and how they relate to individual measurements.

Alternatively, if the room is an empty shell, take the dimensions of your chosen furniture and show them to their exact scale by marking out their shape on the floor using masking tape or chalk. You could even make full-size paper cut-outs and move them around accordingly. Masking tape could also be used on the walls to show elevations.

Drawing Up a Floor Plan

If you are doing up a whole house or tackling a large and complicated room, you will do better to employ a specialist surveyor to draw the floor plans for you. If you simply want a basic floor plan to refer to when revamping a small room, you can probably do this yourself.

Work methodically clockwise from one corner of the room, tackling each elevation (wall) in turn. You can use a steel measure or an electronic one. Work either in metric or imperial (floor plans are usually recorded in metric). Decide which scale you are using – 1:100 is standard. Use scaled paper (the sort with faint squares on it).

If the wall is broken up by alcoves or stepped sections, measure the depth of these and show them clearly. You also need to record heights of fixed features, such as windows, doors, architraving, radiators and skirting boards. These will be added to the elevations (see page 58) and you will need to show the position of power sockets and light switches in relation to them. For clarity, use different-coloured felt-tip pens to signify different items – for example, red for radiators and blue for power sockets.

As well as drawing up floor plans, take as many photographs as possible. The more information you collate, the better. Stand in each of the four corners and take a photograph of the room from that angle. Then repeat when standing centrally against each elevation. Take photographs of all the details of a room, too, particularly awkward or ugly features, such as ceiling beams and radiators.

CHECKLIST: FLOOR PLANS

→ Floor plans convey information such as dimensions and the position of fixed architectural features.

→ They can also indicate the flow of a room and how it can be zoned.

→ The legend box holds additional information, such as the scale to which the plan has been drawn.

→ Always note the scale, paper size and number (of revisions) when reading plans.

→ Any change to a plan must be shared with all members of the building team.

→ Never mix metric with imperial measurements – most plans use metric.

CHECKLIST: SCALE

→ If something is 1:1, it is a full-size replica of the given object.

→ The smaller the second number, the greater the increase in scale.

→ Make scaled cut-outs of furniture in order to plan the space.

→ These cut-outs must be of the same scale as the floor plan.

→ Leave enough space around objects for ease of navigation.

→ Remember, a plan cannot convey height – elevations do this.

→ A plan should show elements of symmetry.

Elevations

The elevation, which is a two-dimensional drawing of the height of a space, can tell you:

> The height of the room.
> The height of fixed features, such as windows, doors, fireplaces, skirting boards and radiators.
> Changes of floor level.
> The drop of pendant lights.
> The position of wall lights, power sockets and light switches.
> The depth of structural features, such as beams.
> Heights of furniture, mirrors and artwork.

An elevation complements the floor plan and gives practical information that the plan cannot provide. It might show that a radiator will be too tall to fit under a window, or that a television will be too high to be viewed comfortably if positioned over a fireplace. It will also tell you whether a piece of furniture is of the right proportions for a room.

Elevations slice up a room like a loaf of bread. For example, you might have one that just shows a window centrally positioned against a wall. A second might show the same wall but with a pair of console tables with mirrors at each side of the window. A third, again of the same view, could show a pendant light dropping down centrally within the room.

Perspectives

Specialist training is needed to draw perspectives, which are line drawings showing the proposed design. Expensive to commission, they are not offered as standard by interior designers, so expect to be charged a significant sum for one.

CGI (Computer-Generated Image)

Most designers today use CGIs rather than commissioning an artist to draw up a perspective. It is a photographic interpretation showing how the room will look once the design is in place. If you can't do CAD (computer-aided design) yourself, you could employ someone to produce a CGI on your behalf. Although an additional cost, it is not as expensive as a perspective would be.

CHECKLIST: ELEVATIONS

→ The elevation shows the height of a room and the objects within it, including furniture, lighting and art.

→ Elevations should be read in conjunction with floor plans – the two together give the total picture.

→ Elevations are marked by different letters (starting with A) to save confusion.

→ Think of the room as a sliced loaf, with each slice (elevation) denoting a different viewpoint of the same wall.

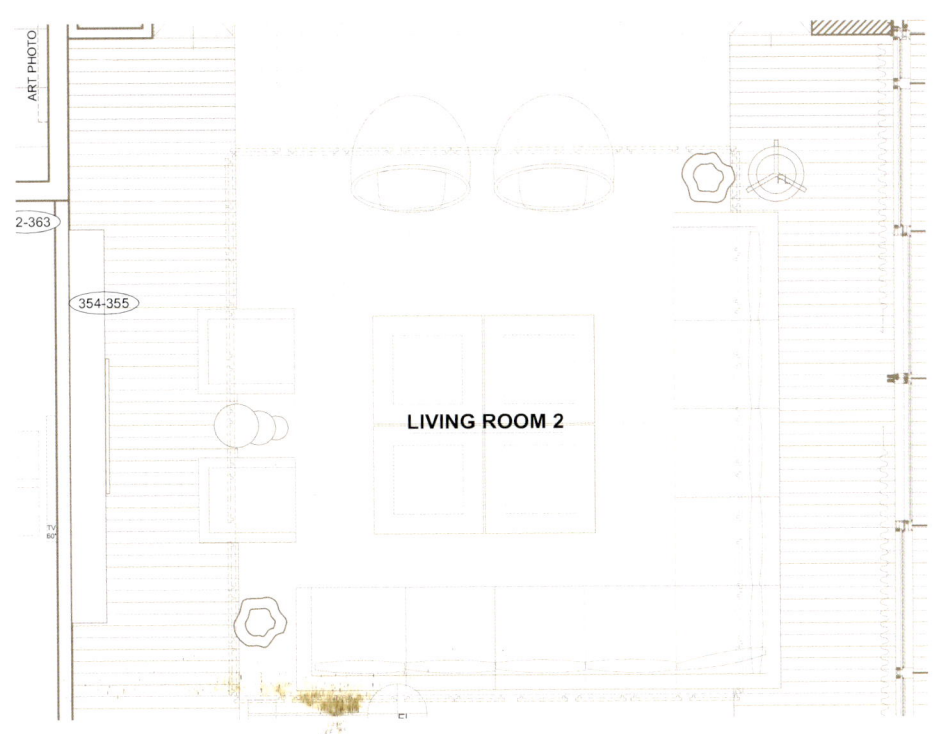

This page and opposite *The floor plan (left), elevation (opposite) and CGI (below) produced for this elegant interior. While the plan gives a clear bird's-eye view of the layout, the elevation (part of a series 'sliced' at different points within the room, this one drawn from just in front of the Bubble-style chairs) is key to understanding how the room will actually look and function. Once the elevations have been signed off, it is possible to produce a CGI to accurately depict the final scheme, complete with colour palette.*

DESIGN CONSIDERATIONS

THE BONES OF GOOD DESIGN

While it is important to allow your mind to wander freely in a creative sense, it is also important to recognize that there are certain factors to consider when designing an interior. The physical advantages and disadvantages of the space are one constraint; the needs of the people who inhabit that space are another; budget is a third; time a fourth. The biggest influence, however, will be your own sense of aesthetics. While this is often defined as a certain way of *seeing* things, it is just as much about how a room enhances *mood*.

It helps if you can develop an awareness of the many layers that go into a room. That does not just mean the many decorative ingredients, such as paint, carpet, fabric, lighting and furniture. It is about the aspects of design that are more intangible: symmetry and balance, scale and proportion, creating impact and interesting juxtapositions.

Opposite Everything in this calm, controlled dining space has been beautifully thought through, from the hand-crafted, ceramic Blossom lights by Jeremy Cole to the Fontana-style slits on the dining chairs' upholstery. The pleasingly symmetrical bones of the room are underlined by structural elements, such as the twin doors at the far end, and decorative touches, such as the row of white roses down the centre of the taupe-lacquered table.

THE DESIGN CONCEPT

Good design is about focusing on the overall effect of different materials and colours, rather than becoming obsessed by individual elements. Before you tackle the question of how the room you are designing will *look*, take time to consider how you want it to *feel*. Forget fabric swatches and paint samples – back to those later – and gather around you images and textures that make you feel happy. Try to capture the sort of mood you would like to reflect in your home. Pin them all together onto one board.

This sort of concept board can include any inspiration you like: art postcards, travel photography, lifestyle elements such as cookery or gardening, fashion shoots, jewellery detailing or swatches of vintage fabric. Together these create a visual reminder of what you would like to achieve in this room. The concept board is a benchmark you can return to again and again, so that you do not lose sight of your original inspiration. Do not confuse it with a design board, which is a breakdown of the actual decorative scheme, showing everything from wallpaper, paints and fabrics to furniture shapes, upholstery and accessories.

It helps if you feel relaxed when you are designing. Allocate a good chunk of time to the process, put on some music you love, take some deep breaths, and enjoy. Creating your perfect home should be a pleasure, not a penance.

IN DETAIL
THE ELEMENTS OF DESIGN

00 Every room should adhere to certain principles.

01 Walls, ceiling and floor create the basic canvas against which everything is set, as with the specialist plaster finish here used to display art and treasured objects.

02 Symmetry is a highly effective tool. The alcoves on each side of the fireplace have been fitted with glass shelves for displaying old leather-bound volumes.

03 Provide balance through different forms and textures. Here masculine velvet armchairs are juxtaposed with a smaller pair in an embroidered geometric print.

04 Make use of scale, both large and small, as with the antique barometer hung next to the large oil painting.

05 Break the rules by introducing something unexpected. These tall, glass display units are an inspired choice for a collection of antiquarian books.

06 One or two star pieces make an impact. This crystal-and-bronze pendant light is the centrepiece around which all pivots.

Right A different view of the room shown on page 54, this time looking from the dining room to the main seating area. This elegantly controlled scheme illustrates how old and new can be persuaded to work together in perfect harmony. A collection of antiquarian books, a rare antique carpet and magnificent Old Masters have been cleverly integrated into a scheme that also includes contemporary armchairs, an AV system, bespoke glass display cabinets and floating shelves. The crystal-and-bronze lights by Mark Brazier-Jones are a key feature, bridging, as they do, traditional craftsmanship and a modern design aesthetic.

THE BONES OF GOOD DESIGN | 65

Symmetry and Balance

If you are lucky enough to have a room that is beautifully symmetrical, then half the battle is won. In truth, few of us are that fortunate. To improve symmetry, use the idea of the grid within design (see page 44), emphasizing the vertical and horizontal planes to add a sense of order. Try to place a focal point centrally – such as the bed within the bedroom, or the table within the dining room – and work out from this. Vertical lines may be accentuated through high-backed chairs, tall vases or floor-standing lamps. The horizontal might be underlined through low tables, artwork in 'landscape' frames or wide pendant lights. Use the grid system to draw attention to those items that are matched by another item – for instance, a pair of console tables, mirrors or chairs. In this way, you will achieve a sense of symmetry even in a room of less than perfect proportions.

However, do not restrict yourself to only two of everything. You will end up with a room that looks very dull and predictable if you take the idea of symmetry too far. It is also important to add one or two items that stand alone asymmetrically within the scheme, perhaps an amazing vintage light or a fabulous piece of bespoke furniture. Balance is just as important as symmetry, so make sure that such pieces find a visual echo within the room, whether through colour, texture or form. Think of it as the subtle link between the various design ingredients.

Right Symmetry is an important tool in this monochromatic interior, with boldly defined runners of stained wood on the wall, echoed in the lacquered console table with its bronze bar. It is there to form a strong foundation on which less symmetrical objects can be positioned, notably the sleek grand piano and the orrery-style central light by Roll and Hill, with its cluster of globes playing against the linear structure inherent in the design.

00 IN DETAIL
SYMMETRY AND BALANCE
These should be at the heart of a room's layout.

01 Consider how symmetrical the room is and play to its strengths. This room has been furnished so that one side is almost a mirror image of the other.

02 Buy key pieces of furniture in pairs. This super-size room accommodates pairs of sofas, lamps, coffee tables and ottomans.

03 Even the way cushions are arranged should add to the symmetry in terms of shape, size and embellishment.

04 Always find a way to then break it up gently. Here, three small cream-lacquered drum tables play against the lines of other furniture.

05 Balancing objects in a display is a talent, made easier here by these glass niches. Choose one type of object for greater impact.

06 Use the grid to underline symmetry, as with the runners on these tables that echo the lines of the floorboards.

Below In a room as large as this, it is important to reflect the different zones within the plan. The main seating area here is designed around a pair of sofas facing each other over a pair of identical coffee tables, topped and tailed by a day bed and a pair of ottomans. Two further seating areas are indicated by identical groups of armchairs and ottomans, but with different choices of table. Circular tables punctuate each end of the room, while the display column is indicated by the double square.

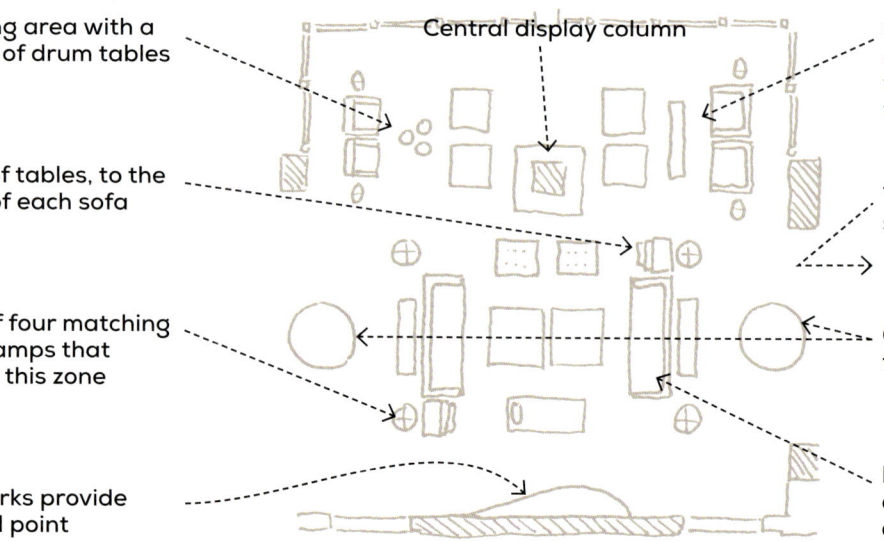

- Seating area with a group of drum tables
- Central display column
- Seating area balancing the one on the opposite side of the room, but with a long coffee table instead of three tables
- Nest of tables, to the right of each sofa
- To the less formal seating area, shown opposite bottom
- One of four matching floor lamps that define this zone
- Circular display tables bookend the main seating area
- Artworks provide a focal point
- Primary seating area with pairs of sofas, consoles, coffee tables and ottomans, plus a day bed

68 | DESIGN CONSIDERATIONS

Above Symmetrical arrangements of furniture are one of the most effective ways of imposing a sense of structure onto a room, evident here in the layout of sofas, tables, lamps and ornamental vessels.

Right In a room designed predominantly around rectangles and squares, it is important to break up the rigidity of line with circles, as with these Bubble-style chairs. These are echoed in the curve of the lampshade and the tabletop arrangement of cylindrical glass vases in the Kelly Hoppen tables.

Scale and Proportion

Over-scaling is another wonderful way of improving the intrinsic architecture and ambience of a room. Again, it relates back to the grid system (see page 44), accentuating either the vertical or horizontal lines within the room. The great thing about over-scaled designs is that you need only one or two to make an impact. Indeed, it is the very fact that the rest of the room sits nicely in proportion that gives over-scaled pieces their theatrical presence. Think of a double-height headboard over a bed, a magnificent antique armoire or a gigantic floor-standing mirror – each becomes a dramatic focal point in a room of similarly scaled objects.

What is less well recognized is the use of under-scaling, which is also a useful tool because it adds a note of wit. The under-scaled object does not shriek for attention, but when it is noticed it gives the observer pleasure of a different kind – that of recognizing the detailed thought process that has gone into the space. Under-scaled objects should link in a subtle way to other items within the room, through form, colour or texture. Think of a single perfect bloom in a clear glass vase, for instance, that is reflected in a nearby extravagant floral arrangement, or mother-of-pearl buttons on a single cushion that reference a runner of mother-of-pearl in a dark wood screen. When positioned well and lit beautifully, miniature objects give just as much pleasure as their over-scaled cousins.

Right This spectacular Avico suspension light by Fontana Arte is not just a source of illumination but also a sculptural centrepiece within this kitchen (see page 209). By keeping the dining table as simple as possible and scaling it to complement the light, nothing diminishes from its impact. Unobtrusive tub dining chairs are upholstered in glazed linen. The only other focal points are the hand-made clay bowls on the table and the collection of white matt ceramic vessels.

Below A collection of small-scaled objects can be just as impactful as large ones, demonstrated here by the green-grey vases displayed in clusters with a white tulip in each. The table is made from cast- and hand-polished hard plaster with integrated lighting. On it stands a glass sculpture Frozen Water by Amanda Brisbane.

Opposite Three gargantuan metal pendant lights by Caravaggio dominate the dining area of this family kitchen. The Tom Dixon Wing chairs at each end of the table also play with the idea of scale, being deliberately partnered with low-backed Wishbone chairs. Low glass vases of moss and succulents echo the circular shapes of the lights above. The table is a linear counterfoil to the curves of furniture, accessories and lighting. It has been stained on site to match the oak floor exactly.

Creating Impact

Our homes are not just personal places where we eat, sleep and unwind. They are also a public display of our tastes and interests. One of the pleasures of creating a beautiful home is enjoying the reactions of visitors, particularly when they are presented with a 'Wow!' moment. Whether we admit it or not, we hope to create an effect that is more than just bland good taste. Great design is also about making an impact.

Every room needs a visual surprise or two. When putting together your scheme, layer on a sense of theatre. The star of the show might be a sumptuous fabric, an extravagant surface finish, a piece of bespoke furniture, striking artwork or any other special object. It might take the form of a jolt of bold colour, a wonderful texture, an over-scaled shape or a vintage one-off. What matters is that you love it and are happy for it to take centre stage.

If you want to use such a piece for maximum impact, place it in such a way that it can be seen from other areas within the house – creating internal vistas is key to creating a wonderful home. Or you might prefer to give no indication of its presence until someone walks through the door, increasing the sense of drama. Think not only of where it is best placed within a room, but also with what it should be juxtaposed to increase its visual impact (see page 78). Build it into your lighting scheme, so that you can ensure it is shown to best advantage at all times (see page 88).

The secret is not to clutter the space with too much else. Star pieces need room to breathe, which is why one per room is usually enough. Think of them as the extroverts of your decorating scheme – the big personalities around which all else revolves.

Left Star pieces of lighting are one of the most spectacular ways of bringing theatre to a space, as with this Kevin Reilly stairwell light suspended from three floors above. Its form and material echo that of the banisters.

Opposite The centrepiece of another sculptural staircase, this specially commissioned crystal chandelier by Spina cascades down two floors, sending shimmering waves and pools into the glass framework. Curved chromed bars, on which hang the owner's antique rugs, echo the contours of the staircase.

Opposite These unusual chairs are the star act of the dining room seen on page 63, their curved backs and crossed legs suggestive of the female form. Upholstered in leather studded with chrome, the back of each is slit, hinting at the work of the artist Lucio Fontana.

Left Rather than hanging this distressed metal chandelier at a conventional height, it was decided to make it even more of a feature within a romantic bedroom by floating it above a circular mirror on the floor. In doing so, it has been transformed into a sculpture.

Below This fabulous floating shelf 'Dune 01' (2007) by Zaha Hadid (Editions David Gill, London) defines the notion of functional sculpture. It is as though a pool of liquid is suspended mid-height.

The Art of Juxtaposition

Layering up a room is not just about choosing an interesting mix of textures, colours and objects; it is also about the effect that all of those things have on each other. That is why successful design does not begin with choosing one paint colour or one upholstery fabric or one chair. In fact, falling in love with a single design and being determined to use it in a room no matter what is often the biggest cause of people not achieving the look they want.

The art of design is about finding a family of textures and colours that will live happily together. Something that may seem inconsequential in isolation can transform into something wonderful when partnered with the right companion. Keep an open mind. Play around with many samples – fabrics, flooring, paint and so on. Look at them in different lights and at different times of the day, and begin to really see what works with what.

Juxtaposition is not so much about things that 'go'. Often it is the opposite – textural contrasts have the effect of bringing out the characteristics of each. A rich velvet, for example, will look even richer and more velvety when placed against a coarse, slubby linen. The gleaming chrome legs of a vintage chair will shine even more brightly against the matt darkness of black-stained floorboards. A crystal vase is better displayed on a rustic driftwood table than on a shiny glass one.

The same applies to the juxtaposition of old with new. Antique and vintage pieces can lift a contemporary scheme to new heights, by injecting the whole room with personality and individuality. In turn, those very pieces often achieve a new life by being set against über-modern materials and finishes. This applies not just to furniture and furnishings, but also to paintings and sculpture. Imagine the impact of a full-scale Tudor portrait in a purist white room, for example, or a classical marble bust adjacent to a collection of provocative twenty-first-century photography.

This page This fine painting looks magnificent in a room that successfully marries contemporary furniture and modern technology with fine art, sculpture and rare objects. Displayed against a textured specialist plaster finish, the red of the little boy's outfit is a splash of accent colour in a scheme designed mainly around shades of taupe and chocolate. To the left, antiquarian books are displayed in bespoke glass floating shelves.

This page Flowering porcelain pendant lights by Jeremy Cole are the centrepiece of this multi-layered lighting scheme. A concealed ceiling recess houses adjustable spotlights to wash light onto art, objets and fabrics. Feature table lamps provide ambient light when dimmed.

LIGHTING DESIGN

Without the correct lighting, even the most expensive and well-considered decorating scheme can appear flat and uncomfortable. Conversely, basic fittings and furnishings can look fabulous if lit well. Good lighting is like a layer of magic dust sprinkled over everything. It affects mood more than any other factor and is not a design ingredient you should skimp on, so make a generous allowance for it within your budget and engage a professional lighting consultant. My own such specialist is Robert Clift.

Successful lighting is all about layers. General lighting should provide enough illumination in a room to create a backdrop for living – it usually means night-time lighting, but can also be used to supplement daylight. Wall and floor washing is a more attractive way of introducing general lighting than the old-fashioned solution of one central pendant. Task lighting focuses on areas where additional light is needed for certain functions, such as reading or sewing. It can also provide navigational lighting, subtly guiding you from one room to another by night. Mood lighting is all about ambience – making a room feel inviting and comfortable. Accent lighting usually applies to highlighting special features, such as artwork, to which you want to draw attention. Star pieces are sculptural lights or installations that strike a dramatic note.

Some lighting sources may be part of the decorative scheme, but remember that what you want to experience is the effect of the light itself. Architectural lighting usually refers to lighting that is not designed to be seen, but that can create some wonderful effects. It is often possible to conceal unsightly spotlights or architectural lighting by creating ceiling recesses and light coffers.

How to Design a Lighting Scheme

Devising a good lighting scheme results in a fair amount of mess and upheaval, with new wiring, relocation of power points and switches, replastering of walls and such like, so it needs to be tackled at the beginning of a room's transformation. As with all good design, it is about building up different layers of light – some for function, others for atmosphere. Plan for more lighting than you may end up using, because the worst scenario is to finish a room regretting that you did not allow for more light sources.

If you are going to tackle the lighting yourself, first plan the furniture layout within each room. This is essential, because where you place sofas, tables and so forth determines where light sources are best positioned. Also, draw up elevations of each wall (see page 58), so that you can see where lighting is needed to complement artworks, collections and other focal features.

You can draw up a simple lighting scheme yourself by photocopying floor plans and elevations and using highlighter pens to show where beams of light need to go. Use pens in different colours – one colour for task lighting, another for mood lighting. Remember, you may want more indirect light sources than direct ones, and that the secret is to 'shoot' light from side to side or up and down. Ceiling lights are often not nearly as effective as those placed on floors or walls. Try to work out where you need 'washes' of light, and where you need sharper, more directional beams.

ROBERT CLIFT'S LIGHTING CHECKLIST

→ Study floor plans and elevations to decide on the furniture layout and the position of key artworks and so on.

→ Remember that indirect lighting can be more effective and comfortable than direct lighting.

→ Build up layers of light, beginning with task lighting and then adding mood lighting.

→ If possible, design a lighting scheme around a number of different electrical circuits, including a 5-amp circuit for lamps.

→ Focus less on ceiling lighting and more on floor and wall lighting.

→ Experiment with different sources of light to bring out the many textures within a scheme.

→ Be generous in the amount of lighting you allow for. It is better to have the flexibility of too much than too little.

→ Be adventurous: some statement lighting does not even have to be a source of light.

Opposite Bronze lanterns with satin shades are suspended at each side of a dressing table to wash ambient light onto the surface below. The under-lit floating unit creates interest, while the discreet LED strips concealed above full-height doors (reflected in the mirror) bounce light onto the ceiling, softening the overall effect.

GENERAL LIGHTING If you position the main light source in the centre of the room, it is likely to cast you into shadow, so instead place fittings, such as floor and wall washers, around the room. You don't necessarily want to direct them towards where the light is needed, as direct light can be very uncomfortable and unflattering. A more effective technique is to direct them towards walls and artwork, so that the room is flooded in indirect light bouncing back into it. Tall units, such as armoires or bookcases, are the ideal place to hide architectural lighting tubes, which cast a soft uplight between the furniture and the ceiling.

TASK LIGHTING Whether it is light you need for reading, for cooking, for applying make-up, or for any other of the myriad functions that take place within a home, you must have strong light sources that enable you to do the things you want with ease. Well-positioned, recessed spotlights are often ideal. Be brave – you don't have to position these in a standard grid formation. Place them where they are actually needed, both for function and for a more dramatic effect when they are dimmed.

Opposite top left A concealed linear LED strip below this window provides a soft wash of background light.

Opposite top right A chainmail feature pendant light by Terzani is the punctuation between stairs and hallway in an entrance hall.

Opposite bottom left Stephane Davidts's linear sconces wash light up and down the walls for a soothing effect.

Opposite bottom right Kevin Reilly's concealed LED strips on the top and bottom of the cupboards wash indirect light both up and down, leading the eye along the corridor. Wall lights (as above) give ambience.

Above left Oriental-style pendants by Kevin Reilly lead the eye through a formal lobby.

Left The Albedo curved table lamp by Lahumière Design is akin to a piece of sculpture.

Right A ceramic Jeremy Cole pendant light is an effective alternative to a bedside lamp.

ACCENT LIGHTING The best lighting brings out every detail of texture within a room. You need to play with lighting against different surfaces to understand how best to complement the matt of velvet or the gloss of glass. The tightness of the beam cast by a spotlight will influence the effect. As a rule, the smaller the artwork or object you wish to highlight, the tighter the beam should be.

Above left Miniature LED uplighters recessed into the timber floor draw out the colour and texture of the metallic gold of this specialist plaster finish.

Above right This glass display unit, custom-built for a collection of antiquarian books, has miniature LED recessed spots fitted both top and bottom. The case itself is silhouetted by concealed wall lights.

Opposite left These 12v halogen cabinet spotlights highlight the textural objects displayed. Linear niches are lit with warm-white LED strips, creating soft pockets of light.

Opposite top right A clear glass pear-shaped lamp on a brass frame.

LAMPS

→ The term 'lamp' does not refer to the table-top variety, but is the correct name for what people often call 'bulbs'.

→ Pearl and frosted lamps have now been discontinued in the UK as part of the energy-saving directive. However, some are still available in different colour temperatures (Kelvins). The best are warm white, which are softer and more welcoming than clear. For table lamps, buy shades with diffusers that will distribute a gentler wash of light.

→ LED retro-fit lamps use less energy and are also available in different colour temperatures: 3000k is equivalent to 'warm white', but opt for 2700k or 2500k for a really cosy effect. Such LEDs are particularly effective when under-lighting 'floating' units or shelves. LED light sources can be dimmed, but not in the same way as regular tungsten lamps, so take advice from an electrician.

LIGHTING DESIGN | 87

STAR PIECE There is another layer of lighting to consider: the 'Wow!' moment, decorative piece – whether it is a spectacular central chandelier, a vintage treasure or a sculptural statement design. Such lighting may, in fact, not be a source of light at all, but, instead, be illuminated from external lighting sources, such as spotlights – the idea being to focus on its beauty as an object rather than as a light. Imagine you want to hang a chandelier over your bath, for example. Safety regulations decree that this cannot be wired for use, but you could hang one anyway and create the same glamorous, dazzling effect by washing it with light from recessed spotlights positioned above.

Clockwise from left Perspex rods lit from above with concealed miniature LED fittings make a spectacular centrepiece for this indoor swimming pool. Cascading crystal fittings suspended over a bedside table add glamour and theatre. Hand-blown glass bubbles make a spectacular lighting installation by Melogranoblu in a dining room. Floating display cabinets lit from the top and bottom with mini LED fittings wash the glass vases in pools of golden light. Hanging bedside lamps from Bocci; each sphere is lit by one LED. A white bronze floor lamp with a silk shade becomes a star piece in this sumptuous living room. Integrated uplighters on the base of a glass display unit emphasize the patina of rare antiquarian books.

Above In a yacht with many reflective surfaces, it is highly effective to bounce light off the ceiling, adding an illusion of height and depth. Organic-inspired table lamps in milk-white Murano glass on each side of the two sofas wash soft hues of light onto the display areas and side tables. When dimmed, the combined circuits create a particularly pleasing effect in the evening.

MOOD LIGHTING Nobody wants to live in a house where they are blinded by light. For this reason, you need layers of mood lighting that are conducive to relaxation and conversation. One of the best ways of achieving this is to instruct your electrician to incorporate a 5-amp circuit within the room for table lamps and floor lamps. Not only does this enable you to switch all the lamps in a room on or off from one switch, but it also lets you dim them as appropriate. The most basic improvement you can make to existing lighting is to fit dimmer switches, so that you can alter the mood of a room instantly and with ease. Use soft shades or natural linen for a warm, comfortable feel. If possible, use diffusers with the shades that wash light onto the ceiling.

Above left The Confession Apparatus lamp by Fadi Mansour is a witty design that plays on the idea of intimacy by inviting secrets to be shared via the brass cones on the electric cable.
Above right Traditional table lamps can add a sculptural touch to a room, as with this brass block design with black silk shade.

LIGHTING DESIGN | 91

KELLY'S TOP TEN LIGHTING TIPS

01 Always allow for enough 5-amp power points within your lighting scheme. Position them in corners or close to the chimneybreast. Floor canisters at each side of the fireplace will add instant drama, or they can be placed to wash light onto your window treatments.

02 Search out retro-style pendant lights to create a stunning feature in a room. Don't necessarily hang them centrally – it is more adventurous to hang them low in one corner.

03 Use LED shadow-gap lighting on skirtings and stairs to guide you through the house.

04 In dark basement rooms, try bouncing light off the ceiling to counteract dull days.

05 Direct recessed ceiling lights towards walls to highlight artworks and specialist finishes.

06 Instead of bedside lamps, hang two feature pendant lights on either side of the bed. Mini flexi-arm reading lights can be positioned on the headboard.

07 In a kitchen, you need to be able to switch from a functional look to one that is more suitable for entertaining, so make sure you have a number of circuits. Feature pendant lights hung low over islands or dining tables look fabulous.

08 Highlight trees and special features outside with simple spike spotlights.

09 Ceiling lights directed downwards are harsh and unflattering. Create arcs of light instead by directing light onto the walls and softening it with sand-blasted diffusers.

10 Allow for a pre-set system in your budget, which will fade different circuits in and out for a variety of looks and moods.

Above right A row of antique brass globe lights are a striking choice for a kitchen setting.

Right Miniature reading lamps are combined with a soft wash of light concealed on the underside of floating bedside cabinets.

Opposite Pools of light wash onto the reflective black steel surface of this pair of safes, creating a silhouette effect.

The Whole Effect

The important thing is to be creative, adventurous and imaginative when it comes to lighting. Professional lighting schemes usually incorporate a number of different circuits within one room to provide maximum flexibility and controllability. For example, there might be a 5-amp circuit for lamps; a circuit for task lights; a circuit for wall and pendant lights; a circuit for low-level lighting; and one for highlighting art and other star pieces. These different circuits, each of which can be dimmed or brightened, create many different effects and moods according to which are combined at any given time. Add to these the romantic effect of candles or firelight, and it is amazing how a room can change in character from one hour to the next.

Finally, do remember that pools of shadow can add another evocative dimension to a room's atmosphere. Lighting is not just about light, but about the contrast between light and shadow. Take inspiration from the latest wave of beautifully designed hotels, bars and restaurants that manipulate our moods – calming us down and encouraging us to relax – through the ingenious use of lighting.

Opposite top and bottom Layering the lighting is essential in a large room, so you must include an adequate number of circuits to achieve the look and feel you want. The plan shows the thought process that lighting designer Robert Clift has put into action. The coffer in the ceiling provides a place for indirect general light, and other circuits – such as the 5-amp one for lamps and recessed spots for accent lighting – provide depth of mood and comfort.

IN DETAIL
A LIGHTING SCHEME

The bigger the room, the more important it is that a scheme includes layers of lighting, both functional and ambient.

01 Plot all your furniture positions first. This will enable you to inform your electrician where 5-amp points for lamps and floor lamps must go.

02 Create a light coffer to house a warm-white LED strip so that light is bounced up onto the ceiling for a softer, indirect lighting effect.

03 Always incorporate a circuit to wash light over your window treatments to draw out the textures and colours.

04 'Paint with light' by allowing for enough lighting to fill a room. Lamps or floor uplighters add ambient light to a large space.

05 Lighting is a crucial aspect of display. These niches have been lit with concealed warm-white LED strips to silhouette display areas.

06 Position recessed ceiling spots so as to highlight specific areas, giving drama and depth to feature pieces. Add candles to enhance the mood.

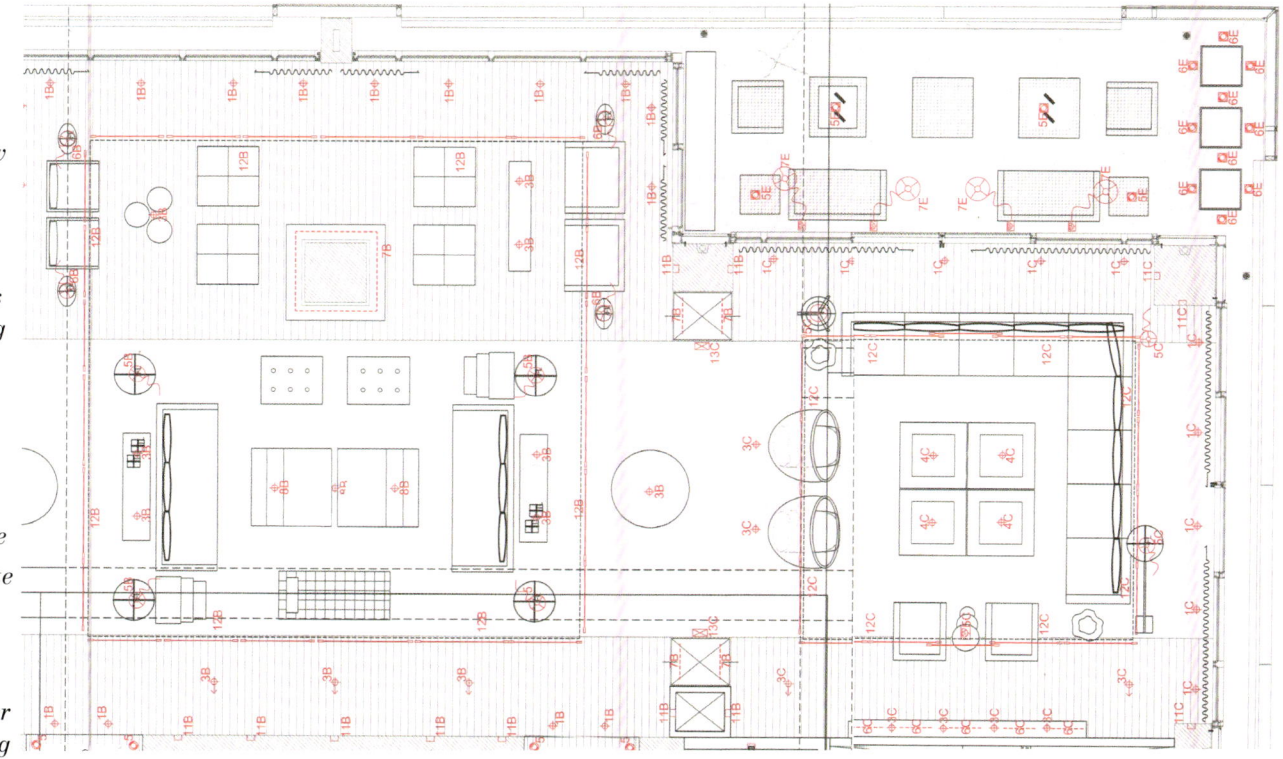

KEY

1B *Recess downlights – for highlighting window treatments*

5B *5-amp points – for lamps*

8B OR 3B *Recess spots – for accenting*

11B *Low-level circuit – for floor-washing effects*

3B *Directional recess spots – for emphasizing texture*

7B *LED warm-white linear strip – for 'floating' effects*

12B *Indirect lighting within coffer – for general lighting*

LIGHTING DESIGN | 95

WALL AND FLOOR FINISHES

Walls

The first consideration is whether you want the walls to recede into the background or stand out as objects of interest. To a certain extent, this depends on what you are planning to hang on them or place in front of them. There is no point in walls 'fighting' for attention with artwork, so it is best to keep them relatively neutral unless you want the walls to be a feature in their own right.

If you are planning on using paint, buy sample pots and try them on each wall in the room. It is fascinating and amazing to observe how different the same colour can look within the same space, depending on the time of day or year.

Specialist plaster treatments are highly effective on walls, providing a textural finish that is both subtle and beautiful. Not only can plaster introduce a hint of pattern, but, like paint, it offers the choice between a very matt finish or a highly reflective one. Create contrast by setting glossy objects against a matt wall, or opaque ones against a shiny, shimmering one.

Walls offer huge scope to play with texture and colour, whether you clad them in stone or brick, wallpaper or tile them, wax or lacquer them, line them with leather or fabric, or commission a mural. If you long to do something bold but can't blow your budget, consider creating just one impactful wall and keep the other three understated.

Walls are a key feature on which to emphasize the grid (see page 44), perhaps by using a contrasting material running vertically up a wall. This can also improve the proportions of a room – a vertical line will make a ceiling appear higher, while a horizontal one can make a room seem bigger. If the room has an unsightly feature that you want to minimize, draw attention away from it by creating something bold and striking on an adjacent wall.

Previous spread, left The view of an entrance hall through black slatted room dividers, with a black timber runner set into stone. On the left is a wall-hung mirror on a leather strap. The prints are from the Kelly Hoppen Crystal series.
Previous spread, right A lava-stone ledge wraps around the polished plaster walls of this spectacular living room, accentuating the alcoves filled with rare artworks and other collectables.
Above right This black, combed-plaster finish creates depth and mood.
Opposite top The caramel tones of this textured plaster wall finish create additional richness.
Opposite bottom The golden brown of the geometric textured plaster finish in this pool room contrasts well with the stone mosaic edging.

CHOOSING WALL FINISHES

→ Ask yourself whether you want your walls as background or foreground.

→ Do they need to be a backdrop to artwork?

→ Let your budget guide you – paint is cheap, but a finish such as gold wax may be prohibitively expensive. Don't choose anything you may become bored with.

→ Remember the importance of textural contrast – whether the gloss of polished plaster or the matt of dark paint.

→ Avoid lavish patterns unless you wish them to be the star of the room.

→ Experiment with samples of paint and other finishes, studying their effects on different walls throughout the day.

→ Don't be afraid to use strong colour.

→ Make sure that lighting does not pick out the flaws on a wall – paper or fabric are a better choice than paint on a badly plastered surface.

→ Use grids, such as contrasting runners of colour or of a different texture, on walls to improve the proportions of a room.

→ Unless you live in a historic house with beautiful architectural detailing, there is no reason to draw attention to a ceiling. It is better to continue a wall colour over a ceiling (unless you have chosen a very dark or vivid shade) rather than paint it uniformly white. A one-shade base colour provides a foundation onto which everything else can be added.

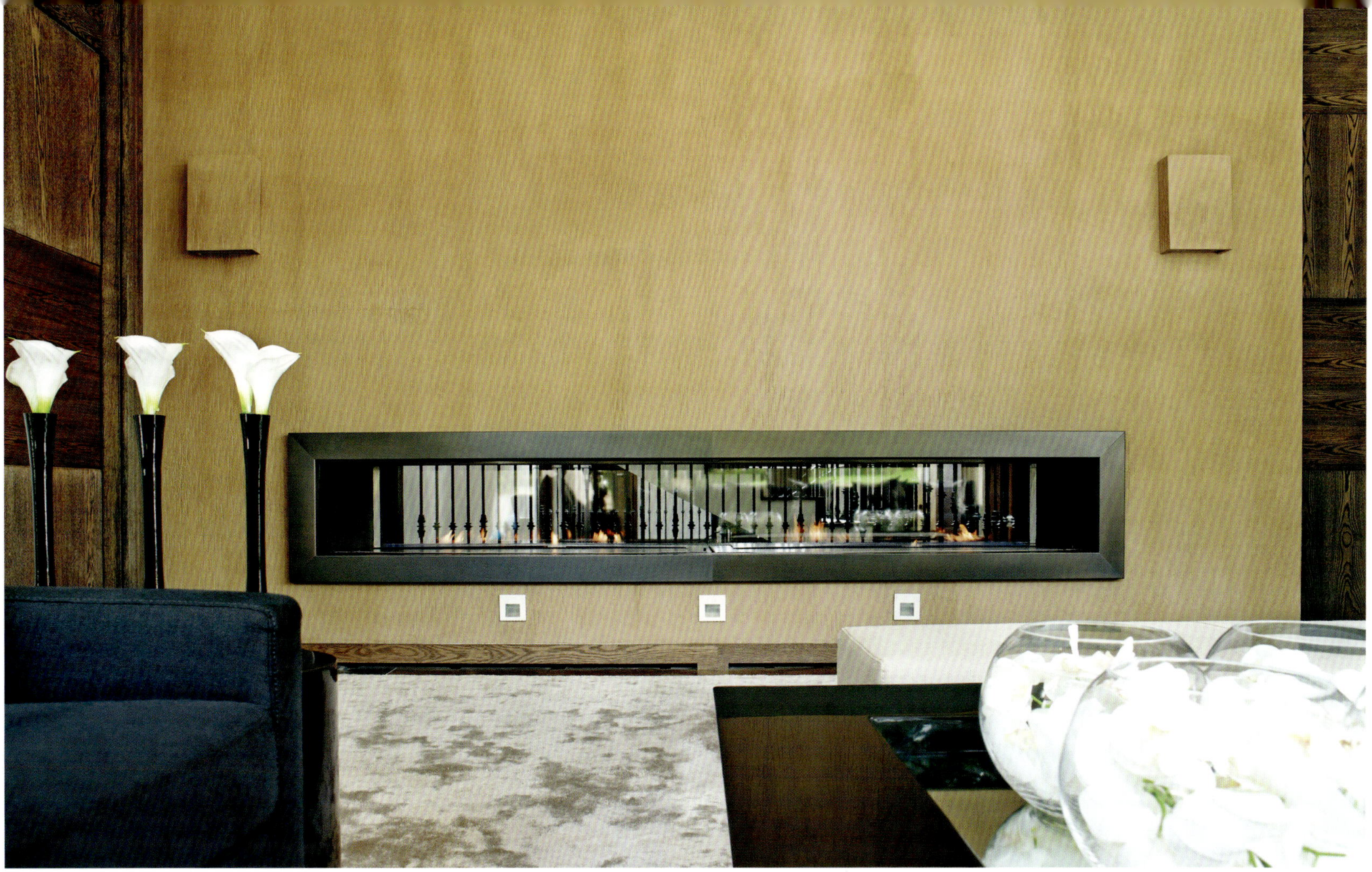

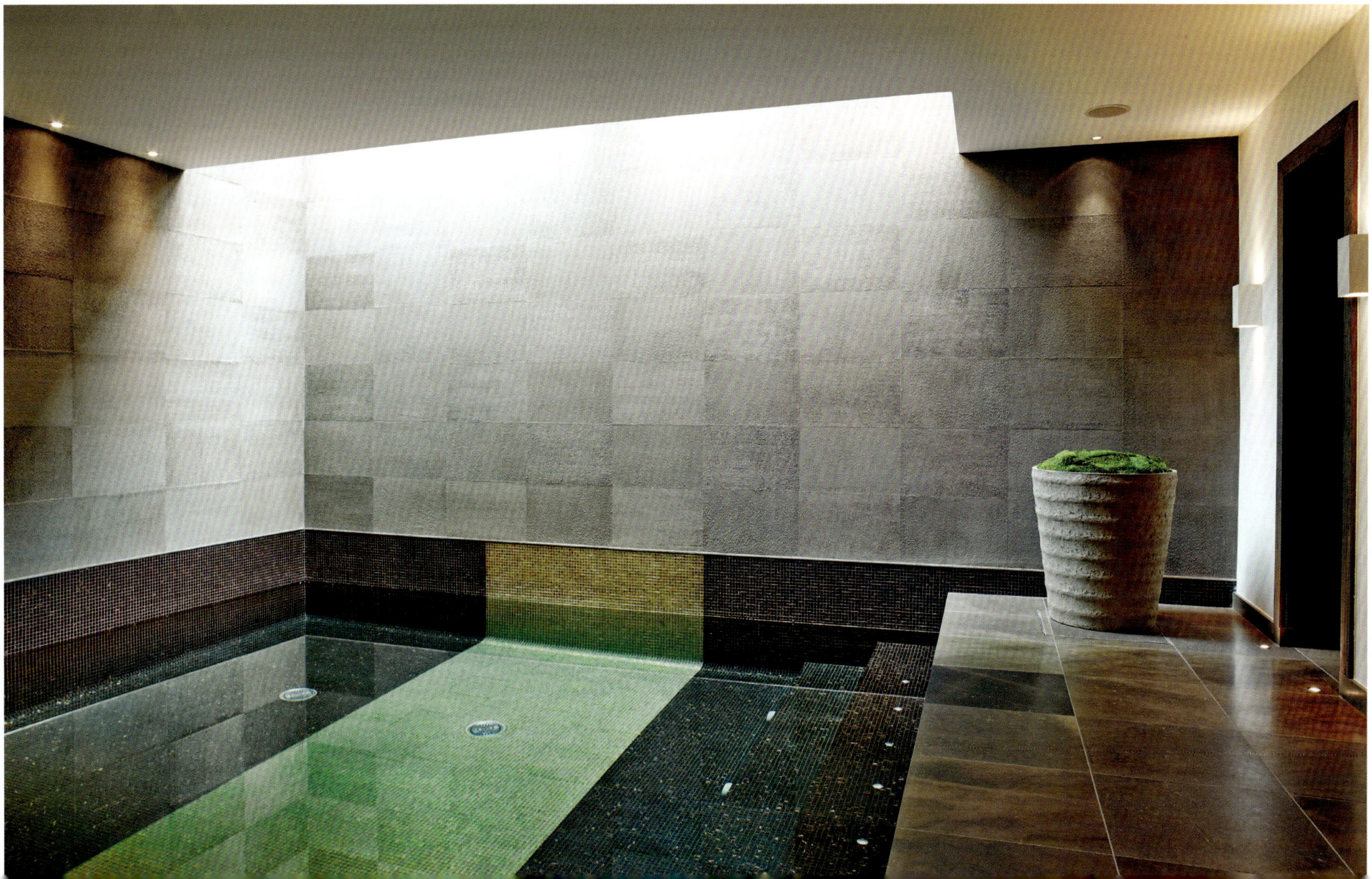

Floors

While some people choose floors almost before anything else, in many ways it makes sense to leave them as one of your final design choices. Once you know the textures and colours of furniture, soft furnishings and wall finishes, you can choose a floor that will be the foundation of the whole scheme. It can also provide a final layer of textural contrast and interest, particularly in relation to walls.

The core decision is whether you want a hard floor or a soft one. Wood, stone and brick floors come in myriad choices of texture, pattern and colour, all of which inject very different moods and looks. However, you should always take advice on maintenance before installation. One spilled glass of red wine can do more damage to a white marble floor than to a silk-carpeted one. It is also essential to employ an installer with skill and experience. If you have specified a runner of dark walnut to be inset into a creamy limestone, for example, it is imperative that both are cut and finished to perfection. Underfloor heating works better with stone floors than with wood floors but, again, take advice on suitability before installation.

Soft floors are equally broad in their choice of weaves, piles, materials and textures. On the whole, they are a less expensive option – a quick way of giving a room a whole new look and feel. Natural fibres, such as sea grass and coir, have a universal quality that suits almost every style of room. Other natural choices, such as wool and silk, also imbue a room with warmth, luxury and comfort. Leather floors are expensive to install but age beautifully.

It can be highly effective to juxtapose soft floors with hard ones, whether runners laid over a timber floor or a section of carpet cut into a stone one. The important thing is to remember that it is not only expensive to change a floor if you get it wrong, but it also creates a lot of upheaval. The best advice is to go for practicality and don't try to make a big statement unless you are very sure about your choice. Having said that, some floor materials are more versatile than others. A wood floor can be re-stained in a way that a stone floor cannot, and if a carpet disappoints, rugs can be added to soften the effect.

CHOOSING FLOORING

- → The floor is one of the largest planes of the room, but it should play a supporting role, not a starring one.
- → Make function and practicality your priorities when choosing a floor.
- → Stone is cold underfoot, but, paradoxically, it is the perfect material for underfloor heating. It is luxurious and durable, but can stain easily.
- → Timber is not only warm and practical, but it can also be painted or varnished to complement your scheme.
- → A brick floor is texturally rich and imbues a room with a rustic mood, but it feels rough underfoot.
- → Leather floors mark and scratch, but this only enriches their natural patina.
- → Carpets are ideal choices for bedrooms, whether it is the glamour of silk or velvet that appeals, or the cosiness of wool.
- → Natural fibres, such as sisal and jute, are a less expensive alternative to wood.
- → Runners and rugs add accents of colour and pattern, and can also be used to emphasize the grid (see page 44).
- → You can introduce elements of both hard and soft within a floor to achieve character and interest.

Opposite top Honed brown stone is the ideal surface for a functional but elegant home spa.

Opposite bottom left A white marble floor with Villi-glass inlay makes a striking foundation to the layout of this bathroom sanctuary.

Opposite bottom centre A wood floor with an inlay of white-lacquered timber makes a bold statement at the core of this living room scheme.

Opposite bottom right Taupe silk-viscose carpet has a rich, glossy sheen that adds a further layer of luxury to this contemporary-styled yacht.

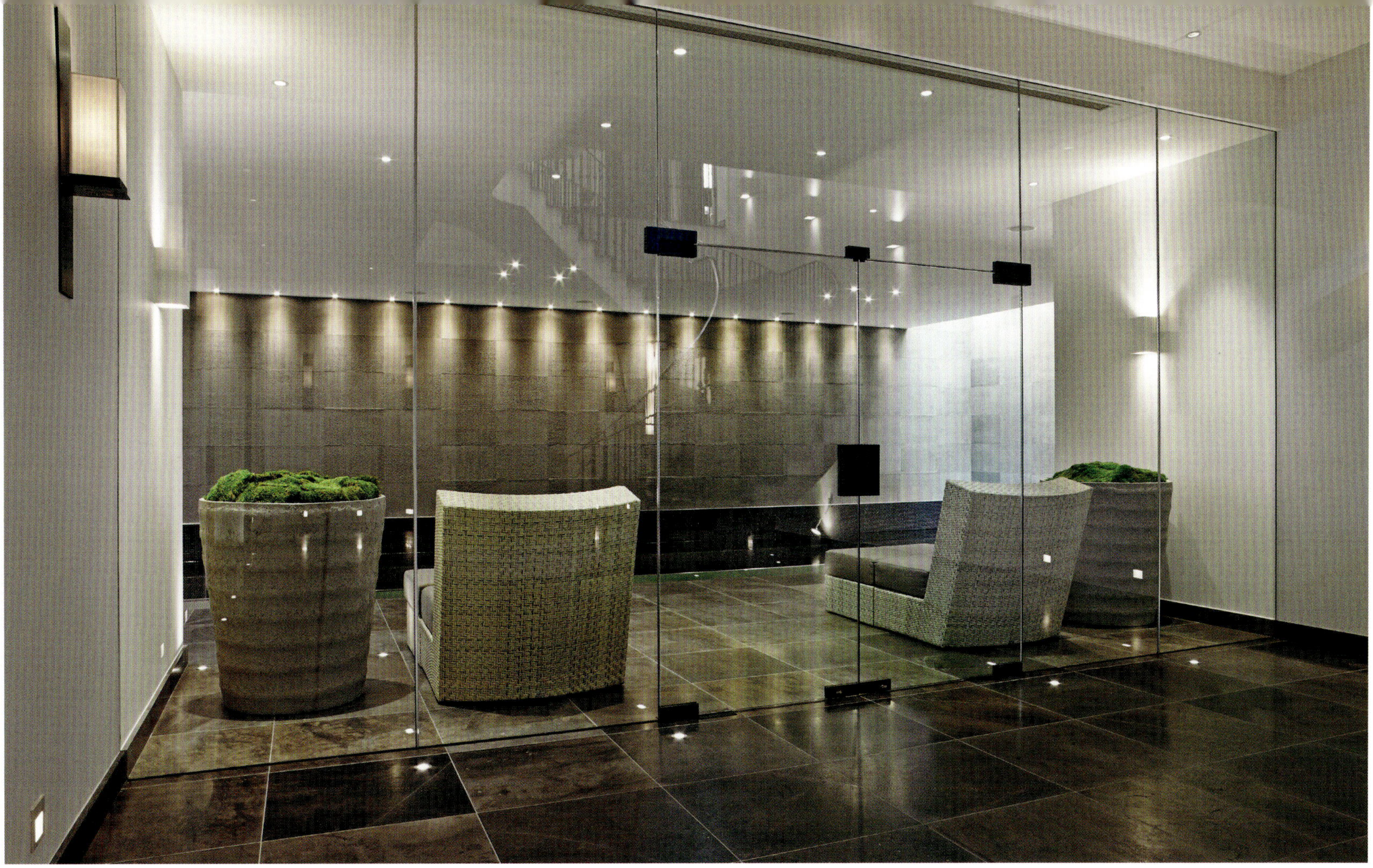

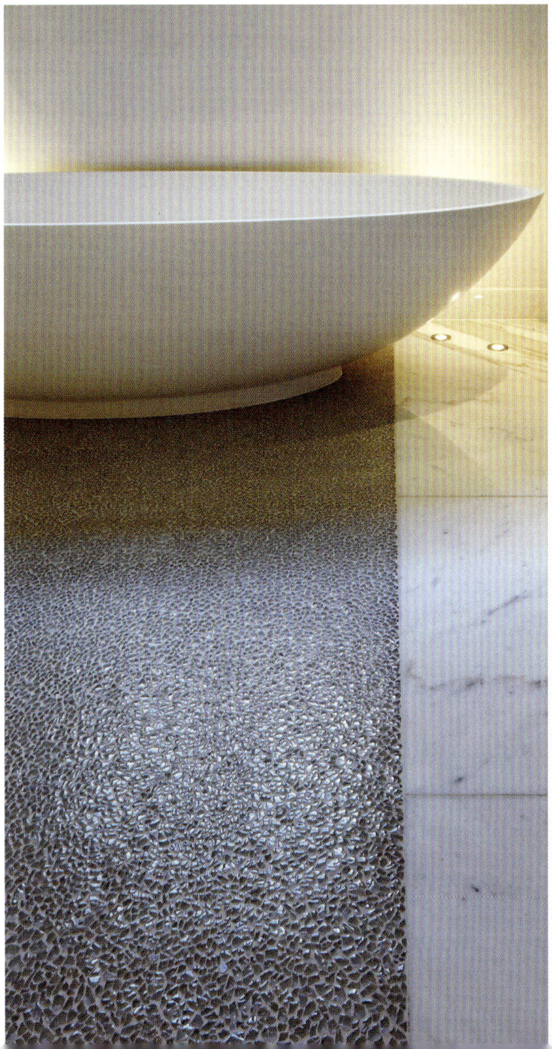

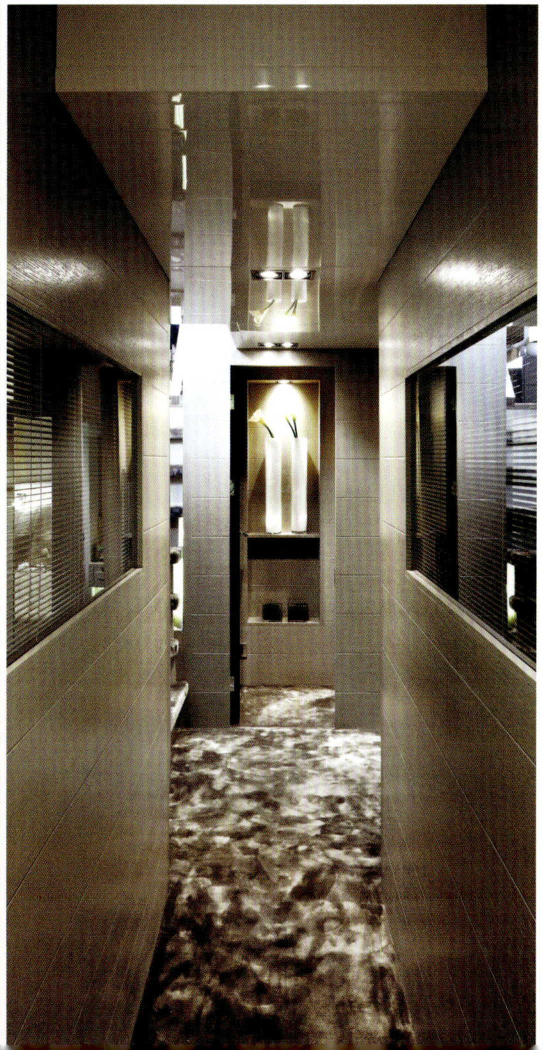

COLOUR, TEXTURE AND PATTERN

When most people think of interior design, they imagine combinations of colours: a 'white' room, 'red' room, 'blue' room and so forth. Certainly colour is one of the driving forces of the decorative side of design, but it makes no sense to consider it in isolation from texture – and, to a lesser extent, pattern. It is also impossible to choose colours without knowing how they will be affected by a property's light – both natural and artificial. There is no colour without light, so the very term 'colour' means nothing without the presence of light.

The big planes of the room – the walls and the floor – are the most challenging to get right because of this. A tiny block of colour on a paint chart might appear perfect, but once it is covering four huge areas within a room, it will take on a very different appearance and character. This is why it is so crucial to collect together as many samples of fabrics and surface finishes as possible, and view them in your own home at different times of day and evening.

If you feel confused by all the choices on offer, begin by looking at your own wardrobe. If you enjoy wearing certain colours, it stands to reason you will almost certainly like living with them. Putting together a room is not so very different from putting together an outfit.

Left A row of over-scaled, silver-painted porcelain vases with unusual dragon ears casts interesting reflections, while also being reflected in the adjacent mirror.
Opposite An architectural column of lacquered timber with chrome-framed niches makes a key statement in a multi-zoned living area. Inexpensive clear glass vases in a variety of shapes are elevated to the status of a decorative collection within this setting.

Colour Palettes

Neutrals provide a quiet and harmonious backdrop against which to live your life. They can also change mood quickly through the introduction of different accent shades, making them practical, versatile and timeless. Creating a neutral, monochrome shell is akin to an artist having a blank canvas. It provides the perfect backdrop onto which fabrics, furniture and furnishings can be added. You can then bring in accents of bold colour or interesting texture elsewhere in the scheme.

It is important, however, to understand the essential differences between two very distinct neutral families: sand and taupe. Sand has an undertone of yellow. Taupe has an undertone of grey and purple. They do not mix and are rarely comfortable together. If sand is the South Pole, taupe is the North.

A popular misnomer is that neutrals are either 'warm' or 'cold'. Whereas sand and cream are always warm, others – such as taupe, white and grey – are not so easy to categorize. To explore this, take the purest white sample you can find and then place different whites alongside it. You will soon start to see how pink, blue, grey or yellow different shades of white become when juxtaposed with the 'pure' version. In fact, no neutral is only ever that colour. Just as there are big variations in whites, so the same is true of other monochromes, such as black and grey.

Finally, while most neutrals tend to fall into the taupe or sand families, there are some that defy logic by working well with either. It is possible to design monochromatic schemes of mixed neutrals – breaking the rules given here – but you need an exceptionally good eye and a confident approach to do this successfully. If in doubt, be guided by the advice on the following pages.

Right Pure white walls, black joinery and the smoky glass of the media wall create a monochromatic canvas for the taupe silk carpet and taupe upholstery. Cushion bands in purple add contrast. The view to the dining room beyond continues the same colour palette.

This page The white-stained floor and white-shuttered sliding doors of this super-size drawing room underpin a scheme that is predominantly white accented with taupe. Pale upholstery and white-banded cushions accentuate the feeling of space and light, creating a calm backdrop for star pieces, such as the pieces of art on the wall and the Zaha Hadid shelf, 'Dune 01' (2007, Editions David Gill, London). Only the red and blue of the artwork by Arman and the green of the plants and moss inject a touch of bolder colour into these cool tones.

Pure White

White-on-white rooms are clean, fresh and energetic. More striking than cream or off-white, pure white brings glamour and a note of drama to a space. It is also remarkably versatile, working well with both sand and taupe. Strong, confident colours, such as navy, red and green make striking accents. White is the ideal choice for sun-filled, southerly rooms full of floaty fabrics, bleached wood, clear glass and cool marble. Pure white is also a dynamic accent colour.

Above Bleached white woods and polished Thassos marble create a foundation for a mix of white linens – the different weave sizes add texture. Silver detailing is apparent in both the hard and soft materials – for example, the polished chrome curtain pole and the silver linen.

Cream

Soft, tranquil and harmonious, cream is the natural partner for sands, browns and off-whites. It also suits more dramatic combinations, such as navy blue, chocolate-brown and black, but introduce them in small doses so they are not overpowering. Cream-on-cream rooms can cloy the visual appetite, so lots of textural contrast is needed to break up the expanse – for example, rich-coloured wood and terrazzo; wool, silk and velvet. The best linens for cream rooms are those with a slight undertone of green. Cream is the ideal choice in light, sunny rooms.

Left A beautiful off-white marble with natural veining is set against cream and natural-coloured linens of different weights and weaves. Textured silk panels can be used as wall or joinery panelling, adding richness to the scheme. Other special touches include soft, silky velvets, smooth oyster-coloured silks and off-white faux-alligator leather.

Opposite The ornate headboard and footboard of the beautifully carved Baroque-style bed are painted cream, imbuing the room with an air of peacefulness. A cream rose stencilled onto the stone-coloured wall behind echoes the floral damask of the bedspread. An accent colour of red has been introduced on the stripes of the linen cushions.

SAND COMPANIONS

- Natural linens with an undertone of yellow.
- Rich, golden woods, such as oak.
- Creamy limestone or yellowy marble.
- Sisals and sea grass.
- Brown leather upholstery.
- Bronze or verdigris light fittings.
- Burnt-orange velvets and suedes.
- Mother-of-pearl and/or ivory detailing.
- Accent glassware in orange or red.
- Flowers such as tiger lilies.

Right The black timber floor and stone walls provide a deep, textural base for runners of yellow-hued stone and complementing leather upholstery.

Far right The textured weave of the sandy natural linen on the sofa bed is complemented by off-white walls, the bronze wall light and the dark linen of the cushion. Accent shades of orange, brown, black, white and pale verdigris are added by the bubble glassware.

Sand

With its warm yellow undertones, sand creates schemes that are cosy, inviting and earthy. Its natural companions are creams, browns and whites, but it also looks dramatic with small quantities of black. Accent it with bronze, burnt orange and verdigris to bring out the richness of these natural tones. Strong, contrasting accents tend to jar with sand.

Above Rich oak, creamy limestone and sisal carpet have been chosen for the floor. A variety of plain and patterned linens adds contrast, complemented by dark-toned suede, leather and plush velvets. Sheer fabrics play against these heavier materials, while mother-of-pearl and bronze detailing provide textural accents.

COLOUR, TEXTURE AND PATTERN | 111

Taupe

Taupe is calm, quiet and easy to live with. Its natural companions are pure white, matt black and nearly every shade of grey. Accent it with silver, clear glass and strong red.

TAUPE COMPANIONS

- Natural linens with a hint of purple.
- Dark-stained woods, such as walnut.
- Rich-toned carpet.
- Grey or blue-hued stone, such as slate.
- Perspex or glass furniture.
- Chrome or crystal light fittings.
- Dramatic red velvets and suedes.
- Silver and/or shagreen detailing.
- Clear glassware.
- Red roses.

Above Smooth taupe marble has been teamed with a rich, shag-pile silk carpet and taupe gloss lacquer. Natural linens in different weights underpin the scheme, including a delicate, sheer, silver linen. Taupe smooth leather and silk mixed with a dark, luxurious velvet add richness and depth to the mix.

Right The taupe of the linen upholstery and velvet cushion bands are the dominant ingredient in this double-aspect apartment, which is accented with whites and creams. The simplicity of the lacquered timber floor juxtaposes beautifully with the sheer silver fabric at the windows.

DOS AND DON'TS OF A MONOCHROMATIC SCHEME

→ Do be led by what is already in situ – if you have a natural oak floor, for example, you need to choose sands not taupes.

→ Do choose a foundation colour onto which other textures and colours can be easily layered.

→ Do ensure you light the room well to bring out the qualities of every ingredient.

→ Do ring seasonal changes by introducing a new set of accents and accessories.

→ Don't assume that all neutrals will work well together.

← Don't layer on too many different accent colours – one will have more impact than three.

← Don't forget the importance of using different textures.

← Don't assume that monochromatic schemes are easy to design – they need a great deal of thought to get right.

Black, Charcoal and Grey

Dramatic shades of black, charcoal and grey are important players in monochromatic schemes. As with other neutral colours, they are surprisingly varied. Grey, for example, can seem almost purple or almost brown, very soft or immensely dense.

These colours may not often form the foundation of a room, but they are extremely effective when partnered with shades of taupe, for instance. They work particularly well with silver – either as a colour or as a material – and are also the ideal backdrop for crystal lights and door furniture. All of these colours are well suited for use in rooms that are used more by night than by day.

Opposite top The dark tones of the black stone walls and matching timber floor provide a foundation for soft leather upholstery, charcoal cushions, a black hair-on-hide ottoman and black-lacquered side tables. The chrome lamp base, cluster of vases and mother-of-pearl buttons add accents of silver.

Opposite bottom In the same room, low-level floor washers highlight the textural surface of tall glass vases and send shafts of light across the timber floor.

Above A backdrop of thin, ribbed plaster complements the grey polished marble with taupe veins. Black-stained timber for flooring and joinery is enhanced by a mix of different textures, including smooth taupe leather, silvery grey herringbone linen, black hair-on-hide and thick-pile velvet. Midnight-blue linen adds further depth.

COLOUR, TEXTURE AND PATTERN | 115

Metallic Accents

Metallics are intrinsic to the neutral palette, because they bring in subtle colour variation as well as textural contrast. Metallics can also be seen as the jewellery of the room – think crystal door knobs, bronze lamps or silvered legs on furniture.

The metallics divide naturally into the families of sand and taupe. Sand works well with bronze, gold and verdigris. Taupe is complemented by silver, platinum and crystal (which should be classed as a metal for this purpose).

Metallic fabrics add instant glamour to an interior, in much the same way as an evening dress transforms your appearance. They also look fabulous when contrasted with matt finishes. It is essential to light metallics beautifully, particularly as they come into their own by night.

Right A specialist plaster wall finish in gold cocoons this cloakroom in luxury, compounded by the runner of mirror and the floor-standing drum basin.

Opposite top left A row of gold-lacquered pendant lights by Masiero adds magic by day, but especially by night, to this sumptuous dining room. The antique gold-leaf-on-iron frames on the wall behind bring additional glamour.

Opposite top right A mirrored fishbowl sits in a chrome-framed niche of this white-lacquered display column.

Opposite bottom left A polished stainless-steel runner plays against the matt texture of the warm-toned timber floor of this yacht.

Opposite bottom right Mirrorball floor lights by Tom Dixon offset this chrome-edged Bubble-style chair beautifully, while the silver cushion adds another metallic accent to the scheme.

Accents of Colour and Pattern

Punchy accent colours can change the whole character of a neutral scheme. Experiment by introducing just one colour at a time to see the effect on a monochrome palette. Accents don't just change the look visually, but contribute to the whole feel of a room. It is important, therefore, that you choose an accent colour that you really love – be it burnt toffee or olive-green. You don't need more than one accent colour in a scheme, as this can dilute the overall effect.

Accent colours are not just vibrant shades of red, orange and so forth. Black can make a fabulous accent colour in a taupe scheme, for example, just as pure white can be a stimulating choice in a sand room.

By and large, proportion is what counts. The stronger and brighter the accent colour, the smaller the areas in which it should be used. Bright jolts of colour have just as great an impact as larger expanses of a more toned-down colour. The ideal accents are those that can be changed easily, such as cushions, flowers and other accessories.

Pattern need not mean huge and flamboyant. It is best used as a quiet layer within the scheme – an unobtrusive check, perhaps, or a barely there stripe. A surplus of pattern would kill the visual impact of textural contrasts and harmoniously grouped neutrals, throwing too much attention onto a single fabric or finish, rather than allowing the eye to enjoy the entire effect. As with accent colours, pattern is best used in tiny doses – for example, a statement vintage chair could be covered in a patterned fabric, so long as it still 'talks' to the other furniture within the room.

Below Antique gold damask cushions add a subtle accent of pattern to a vintage charcoal velvet sofa.

Opposite A specialist wall finish in a grid pattern of golden tones provides textural contrast against black mosaic tiles inset with a runner of gold mosaic.

Above left Rich purple is the perfect accent for a taupe scheme, as with the soft velvet of these cushions juxtaposed with a textured grey velvet bedcover.

Above right A rich mix of linens, velvets and silks in warm pinks, mauves and purples layer this bedroom with comfort. The hues featured on the cushions pick out colours on the splashy, floral-print bedcover for a harmonious result. The painting is by Allan Forsyth.

Opposite bottom left In a chic city bedroom, a linen/cotton stripe in warm taupe and off-white has been used for both the bedcover and cushions. The plain vertical linen band in a toning shade of taupe adds boldness to this smart but relaxed effect.

Opposite bottom centre and right Wool cushions in a combination of simple stripes and classic plaids in soft shades of grey promote rest and relaxation in a home cinema.

COLOUR, TEXTURE AND PATTERN | 121

Texture

You cannot choose colours in isolation from textures. Texture injects warmth or coolness into a scheme, so is vital when creating mood. Because of the way it interplays with lighting, it also has a huge impact on colour. The two have to be considered together. When working with a neutral palette, you need textural contrast to add depth and character to a scheme (see page 78).

Perfecting the Textural Palette

Working with texture means taking a fresh look at the way you design a room. Conventionally, people often begin a scheme by choosing a colour. While this is obviously important (see page 104), texture is of equal significance. Just as you begin playing around with samples of colour when searching for inspiration, so you should spend time doing the same with different textures.

The first thing you will notice is how they play with light. A dark, slubby fabric, such as dense velvet, absorbs light, whereas shimmering silk bounces it back into the room. Secondly, textures impart mood – a coarse tweed conveys a rustic feeling, in the same way that a soft pinstripe evokes an urban one. Thirdly, texture is all about touch – the intrinsic feel of the room. Some textures are warm and cosy, such as suede or leather, while others are cool and glamorous, such as satin or horn.

When building up texture within a room, you need to consider which ones will dominate and which will provide accents. Accents are there to add contrast, just as a vivid colour in a neutral scheme would. If you have a room that is designed around rough brick and plaster, for example, you might want to introduce accents of mirror, silver, cashmere or vellum. If the dominant textures are rare timbers and polished stone, you might prefer accents of sisal, calico, rough concrete or boiled wool (felt).

As with colour, you have to understand proportion and purpose. Don't add in new textures just for the sake of it – they should work as a family, with each one imbuing a layer of its own characteristics. By introducing textural contrasts, you provide a foil for each of them to come into its own. A velvet will look deeper and richer next to the smoothness of glass, just as a vellum will look even more fragile and translucent adjacent to the rough density of granite.

Opposite Runners of marble on the stone walls and floor of this elegantly simple bathroom create a striking focal point. The wrap-around shelf is made of glass, while the window wall is polished plaster. The bath has a matt finish, and the shutters have been lacquered gloss white.

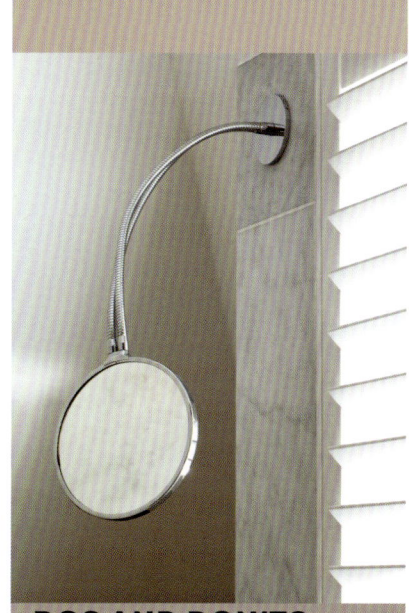

DOS AND DON'TS OF THE TEXTURAL PALETTE

→ Do study the effect of light on different textures.

→ Do consider what type of mood you want to create in the room.

→ Do remember that the same colour can look very different in a range of textures.

→ Do remember that touch is as important texturally as sight.

→ Don't choose too many dominant textures: two or three are enough.

← Don't forget the importance of layering up textural accents within a scheme.

← Don't think you can go too far with the idea of juxtaposition – the more extreme the contrast, the better.

← Don't separate colour choices from textural ones; they are equals.

Above A polished chrome mirror on a flexi-arm is easily mounted on the surround of a window.

Matt and Gloss

This combination of textures is about marrying together objects with different light properties – those that absorb it and those that reflect it. This applies not only to natural light, but also to your room's lighting scheme. It can be something as simple as suede cushions embellished with horn buttons, lacquered doors offset by a brick floor, or a pewter runner embedded into a wenge table.

Below left A Deco-style wall light in nickel complements the taupe of this specialist wall finish of textured plaster.

Below Slot niches with timber bases have been carved into the richly textured plaster walls of this cloakroom. Integrated lights pick out the shiny white surface of the simple ceramic vases.

Below A bespoke laminate panel by Kinon has been used in this dining room both as a grid on the wall and as an alternative to artwork. Its shimmering surface juxtaposes well with the dark oak console and cluster of matt glassware displayed on it.

Below right Surface contrasts abound in this spectacular guest cloakroom, from the mosaic runner set into the timber floor, which travels up the polished plaster walls, to the grid of mirror, which matches its dimensions exactly. The rectangular glass basin sits on a glass ledge.

Rough and Smooth

This defines tactility – the enjoyment of running fingers over different surfaces. It is also about mood – the rustic simplicity of a rough texture with the glamorous luxury of a smooth one. Imagine a tweed throw trimmed with ribbon, silver vessels on a rough-hewn oak table, or calico curtains edged with satin.

Opaque and Transparent

As with matt and gloss, this is all about manipulating light – not through reflection, but through diffusion. It is a softer, more sensual effect that plays on the idea of light and shadow, transparency and solidity. Think of a leather door with vellum panels, screens that combine sand-blasted glass with clear glass, or sheer curtains pooling onto a limestone floor.

Previous spread, left A wall of riven quartzite makes a spectacular focal point in a pool room, particularly with water continually running down its jagged surface. Columns of mosaic provide an unexpected contrast, both of texture and colour.

Previous spread, right The iron-and-brass lamp base of this sculptural floor lamp plays against the linen upholstery with chrome-stud detailing.

Right A white linen cushion with button detailing works well against the reflective surface of an acrylic Bubble-style chair, providing an element of solidity against the transparent material of the chair.

Opposite A collection of jade glassware is lit by sunlight and makes a textural play against the gloss surface of the piano. The carpet is silk, edged with velvet, while the window is hung with warm sateen curtains and a geometric sheer.

Hard and Soft

This focuses on the architectural qualities of a room: making up the bones – the hard lines of doors, cornicing, floors and windows – and then softening them with furniture, fabrics and accessories. It is about feeding the sense of tactility: fine linen curtains juxtaposed with polished plaster walls, jute runners on a wood floor, or bronze table legs against a silk carpet.

Opposite A silver linen sheer curtain plays beautifully against the 'corduroy' finish of the specialist plaster wall.

Above Silver linen fabric walling and matching upholstery combine with silk-viscose carpet to create a soft foundation for the faux-crocodile leather base of the bed and the trunks at each side of the seating.

CABINETRY

When it comes to choosing furniture, one of the first considerations is whether you are opting for bespoke fitted cabinetry or freestanding pieces. Built-in fixtures are part of the internal architecture and have to be planned at the outset. The advantage of commissioning such work is that it can be designed specifically for your storage needs, with customized spaces for everything from DVDs and photo albums to sheet music and champagne flutes. Also, you have the opportunity to choose the materials, colours and finishes that complement your scheme precisely. Cabinetry requires a great deal of skill and is expensive to do well, so you need to budget generously for it. Being part of the internal architecture, you cannot take it with you when you move.

Buying suitable freestanding pieces or customizing ready-made storage systems is often less costly, but nothing beats having furniture made specifically for your home: it is the couture end of design. In addition to being able to specify the materials and finishes, you can incorporate special touches, such as vellum door panels or horn handles. Cabinetry is a way of playing with textural juxtaposition (see page 122), perhaps by combining a dark timber with mother-of-pearl detailing, or marrying etched glass with rich-toned leather. Think of door furniture as the jewellery on the outfit.

Cabinetry is not just about concealment of items – it is about display, too. Because of this, you might want to commission integral shelves or alcoves with integrated lighting as part of the brief. Such furniture is a clever way of camouflaging ugly wiring or AV equipment and, if designed well, it can also be used to improve the proportions of a room. The one note of caution is to remember that whatever timber you choose, it will set the tone of the room – cabinetry in pale ash engenders a completely different mood from heavy oak, for example.

Opposite An oak-veneered display unit matches the timber of the floorboards. The combination of open and concealed storage gives versatility and character, in keeping with the iconic Lounge chair and ottoman by Ray and Charles Eames.
Left Slatted dark-stained wooden walls, lit between the grooves, provide atmosphere and textural depth in a lobby area.
Right A media wall features pull-out drawers of dark wood with contrasting leather runners, making a sleek storage solution in a family home.

Above left and right Two views of the same room showing how an oak-coloured bookcase with a sliding door in taupe plaster has been designed to create different vistas according to which panels are open and which are concealed. Books, vessels and sculpture create interesting tableaux.

Below left The Mondrian dresser from the Kelly Hoppen kitchen for Smallbone is a signature piece that combines open and concealed storage in a variety of materials, including black textured wood, pure black lacquer, silver-leafed mirror and painted basketwork.

Below right Bespoke glass cases have been designed to house a collection of rare, antiquarian books. Here they float against richly textured plaster walls.

Opposite top left In the dressing area of a master-bedroom suite, louvred dark-stained timber doors provide contrast against the pale silk carpet.

Opposite top right Taupe-lacquered dividers on an oak-veneered bookcase add contrasting texture to the matt timber. Cigar sculptures by Arman and crystal glasses from Formia make an intriguing display.

Opposite bottom left The master cabin of this yacht features an integrated dressing table, which has drawers in taupe leather with runners of silver linen.

Opposite bottom right This line of oak veneer closet doors with cut-out handles provides an unbroken vista of the powder area of a large master dressing room.

Doors

The front door, the physical connection between your home and the world, is one of the most important fixtures within the house. It needs to be chosen both for the style it sets from the outside and the sense of security it offers from the inside. If you can afford it, don't buy 'off-the-shelf', because you will be limited to conventional sizes. Enlist an interior designer or architect to help you design your concept door – and, if possible, scale up the dimensions so that it makes a strong statement both externally and internally.

In general, doors look better when scaled up in size, particularly those that lead from the principal rooms off the hall. If possible, have double-height versions that reach nearly to the ceiling, either single or double. If you are designing doors from scratch, bear in mind that there are many ways to build them. A door can pivot, slide or concertina, maximizing the available space.

Very often, people fail to see the potential that doors offer. They are not just a functional necessity, but are akin to wall panels on which you can play with finishes, tones and textures. While most doors are timber or glass, it is also possible to introduce other materials, such as leather, metal, lacquer or studwork to contrast or complement the existing surface. Neither do they have to be solid – you may prefer a door that is opaque with panels of vellum, or slatted like a Japanese screen.

Door furniture is the jewellery of the door, whether hammered bronze, rock crystal, horn, nickel, silvered, shagreen or any one of myriad choices. It can also be designed like runners to echo the grid of the room.

Left A stained oak door with a recessed bronze handle is juxtaposed against the luxe gold of a specialist plaster wall finish.

Opposite, top row left to right Sprayed wooden doors with faux-crocodile panels and D-handles. Oak-veneer door with hand-cast nickel door pull. Stained oak with recessed bronze pull handle. Black-stained door with central groove detail and polished nickel door furniture.

Opposite, centre row left to right A detail of the image shown above right of the textured nickel door pull on an oak-veneer door. Oak-veneer door with over-sized, recessed, polished chrome handles. Stained-oak panelled doors with recessed bronze handles. Glass doors with dark bronze pull handles.

Opposite, bottom row left to right Oak-veneer door with hand-cast textured nickel door pull. Oak-veneer doors with cut-out handles. The same black-stained door with central groove detail as shown top right, here with a bespoke polished chrome door pull.

FURNITURE

Furniture is about form as much as function. It enables you to play with many of the 'bones' of design discussed at the beginning of this chapter (see pages 62–79): symmetry and balance, scale, creating impact and interesting juxtapositions. Other pieces are unapologetically feminine – curvier, softer and more likely to be embellished. It is fun to recognize this and enjoy playing the two aspects off against each other.

While there are certain essentials on the furniture shopping list – such as sofa, storage and dining table – it is a shame to buy furniture only for functionality. You need some pieces that work on a very practical and comfortable level, such as the bed, but it is important to shake things up by investing in one or two pieces that are less about everyday use and more about introducing mood and personality. Occasional chairs are a good way of doing this without blowing the budget. A chair is a naturally sculptural object, which offers a vast number of possibilities in terms of shape, size, upholstery and finish. Just one star chair can be enough to imbue a room with interest and character.

The best furniture layouts are those that include pieces from a variety of sources, so that flea-market finds sit next to inherited pieces, and high-street staples are set against icons of design. Too often people make the mistake of finding one store or designer that they like and buying virtually everything for their home from this one source. The result is a house that looks like a showroom, rather than a home of individuality and wit. Put your furniture together as you would your wardrobe – an intelligent combination of vintage, inexpensive labels and investment pieces.

Previous spread A pair of chrome-edged Bubble-style chairs are a witty addition to the restrained mood created by the L-shaped seating and square white-lacquered tables. Together with a small, organic-shaped side table by Sé in the foreground, they punctuate the linear style of the other furniture.

Opposite This sculptural armchair by Pedrali, made of smoky grey polycarbonate and with a taupe velvet seat cushion, is a star piece within the dining area of a kitchen.

Above right A nest of white-lacquered side tables is a useful addition to any living room where guests are often entertained.

SHOPPING FOR FURNITURE

- Most importantly, make sure it fits. Carry dimensions with you as a reminder of the size needed not only to fit the required room, but also to go through the front door and (if applicable) up the stairs.
- Don't buy everything from one store. The result will be very boring and bland.
- Scour antique shops and flea markets for quirky pieces that can be renovated or re-upholstered to fit with your own style.
- Don't skimp on key pieces, such as beds or sofas, which you do not want to replace too quickly. Always try these out before making a purchase.
- Don't impulse buy. Furniture has the biggest impact on the overall aesthetics of a room, so mistakes are hard to live with.
- Study the form of furniture – is it masculine or feminine? Introvert or extrovert? What mood will it bring to the room?

Above Chrome studs emphasize the lines of these leather-upholstered armchairs from the Kelly Hoppen collection.

Top right Black-lacquered Tam Tam tables are both functional and sculptural.

Above right A high gloss, taupe-lacquered coffee table on a single base by Baltus plays against the soft silk carpet.

Right A contemporary interpretation of the iconic Bubble chair by Eero Aarnio – a classic mid-century design.

Top left A pair of black-stained wooden coffee tables with metallic runners are at the core of a symmetrical seating area.

Left The unusual contours of this Christopher Guy occasional chair were chosen to echo the curve of the adjacent staircase. The black frame and deeply padded sateen upholstery complement the crystal light hanging down from two flights above.

Below left Simple linen-upholstered tub chairs create an informal dining area in a family kitchen.

Above An elegant lacquered centre table with a fluted, silver-plated copper base is the ideal display area for cream ceramic vessels and orchids.

Furniture Layout

Cabinetry (see page 132) is a permanent feature of a room, and the chances are it will be obvious where it should go. What is harder to get right is the layout of freestanding pieces, such as sofas, coffee tables, occasional chairs, bookcases and such like.

If asked to design a furniture layout, most people begin by positioning the big pieces within a room and work out from those. You will achieve more impact, however, if you consider your star pieces first: where will the beautiful, inherited desk go? Or the pair of antique chairs upholstered in Fortuny silk? Or the twenty-first-century, limited-edition console table bought at a furniture fair? Think about where they can be placed to create maximum impact, not only within the room itself but when seen from other rooms as well.

When looking at floor plans and elevations, and deciding how best to position furniture, be driven equally by function and aesthetics. Play around with scaled designs (see page 56) and experiment with furniture layouts that are not as obvious as you might have thought. If you are renovating an existing home, try not to replicate the same layout you have at present. That phrase 'just part of the furniture' exists for a reason: the challenge is to make sure that you don't stop 'seeing' the pieces that you own. Be ruthless: if you have a piece of furniture that is so unwieldy it can only go in one place – thereby determining where everything else can fit, too – then it may be better to send it to auction and start again. Allow yourself to fall in love with something entirely different.

Above all, remember that the grid (see page 44) is at the heart of the furniture layout. The way that you position key pieces of furniture should reinforce those horizontal and vertical planes. Furniture should not be scattered through a room, but be arranged in a composition that you have orchestrated to great effect.

CGI: LIVING ROOM

The main purpose of this CGI was to illustrate the size of the space and how the different zones relate to one another. It was necessary to include as much architectural detailing as possible, including ceiling coffers and the floor-to-ceiling feature column for display. It was also important to give the client an indication of how the space would look when lit. Interestingly for such a large room, the CGI has remained accurate to the finished room (see pages 36–9). All it needs is the addition of accessories, flowers and artwork.

Above A secondary seating area within the large drawing room shown in the CGI opposite features velvet-covered low ottomans and fully upholstered frame chairs in white linen. Cream-lacquered drum stools with black copper bases are juxtaposed with bronze figurative floor-standing lamps from Porta Romana.

Right An additional seating area within the same room is furnished with the same lamps and ottomans. The armchairs are upholstered in a neutral linen, contrasting with the sheer silver linen at the windows.

IN DETAIL
FURNITURE LAYOUT

The way the furniture is arranged affects the whole feel of this inviting living space.

01 Seating is a comfortable combination of sofas, chairs and a stool.

02 The coffee table is large enough to be in easy reach of all the seating.

03 Lights have been positioned over key pieces of furniture.

04 Carpets mark out the seating and dining zones.

05 Side tables are placed to balance each other.

06 Pictures and objects are displayed at a height to be enjoyed when people are seated.

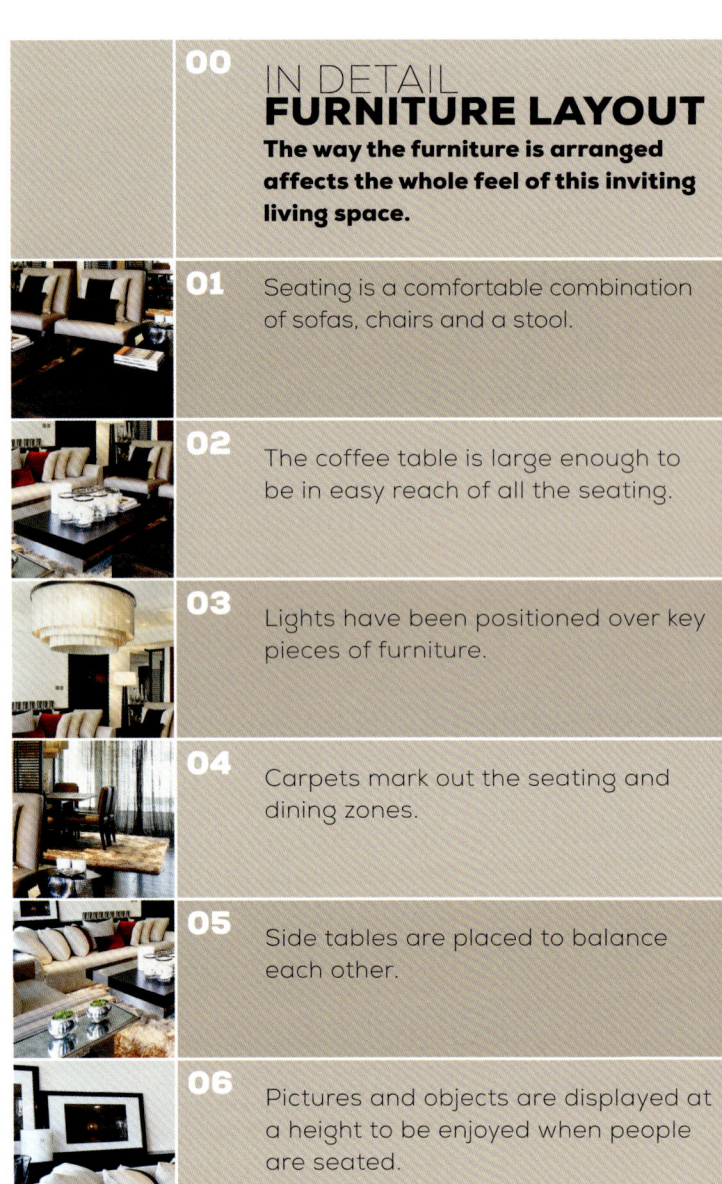

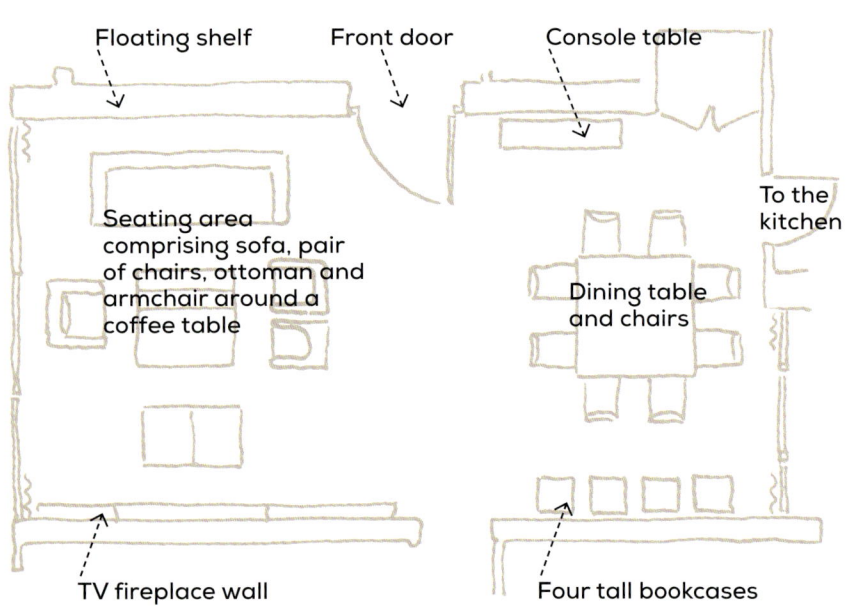

Floating shelf — Front door — Console table

Seating area comprising sofa, pair of chairs, ottoman and armchair around a coffee table

Dining table and chairs

To the kitchen

TV fireplace wall — Four tall bookcases

Left This double-aspect, open-plan space is divided into two zones by the invisible corridor that leads between the doors. The seating area at one end has been designed around a combination of armchairs, sofa and ottoman, with a large coffee table placed centrally. The two side tables in the finished room are a later addition.

Above Floor-to-ceiling, black, slatted screens separate this living space from the dining area beyond. The plan (see opposite) shows how the entrance, in effect, cuts the space in two, creating a division between the two zones. In the living area, the sofa, armchairs and ottoman are cosily arranged around the square coffee table with steel inlay, while a floating ledge behind the sofa provides a display area for artwork and objects. Chainmail pendant lights by Ochre lead the eye to the dining zone beyond. Cushions in linen and velvet soften the dominance of leather. The chairs, table and hair-on-hide ottoman are from the Kelly Hoppen range.

SOFT FURNISHINGS

More than any other ingredient, fabrics denote mood. Consider the laid-back attitude of cotton compared to the dressed-up glamour of taffeta, or the rusticity of wool compared to the luxurious feel of silk. The best schemes incorporate a degree of textural contrast: the slubbiness of raw calico against jewel-coloured velvets, or the matt of suede juxtaposed with frothy lace. Use fabrics to accentuate the grid within the room (see page 44), most notably through banding on curtains, blinds, cushions and bedheads. Bands are akin to runners on the floor – they emphasize the vertical or horizontal planes, while also providing a perfect opportunity to introduce textural contrast.

With so much choice, fabrics can seem a confusing maze to navigate. The secret is to begin with a linen. This grounds a scheme, giving a firm foundation onto which other textures and colours can be layered. Linen is immensely versatile as a fabric – suitable in different weights and finishes for both windows and upholstery – but it is not over-dominating. The most important thing is to select a linen with the right undertone of colour for your chosen scheme. A taupe scheme (see page 112) requires linens with undertones of grey or purple, for example, whereas a sand scheme (see page 110) requires yellowy hues. This acts as a key for all the other fabrics you select.

Once you have found a family of fabrics that you love, you can begin allocating each one to a different purpose. Functionality is a consideration here: upholstery fabrics need to be much more hard-wearing than those used at windows, for instance. You also need to think about how a fabric moves and hangs; whether you want it to block light or filter it; and whether it will be embellished in any way, such as banding, stitching or buttoning on cushions. As a rule, use textured neutrals for big items of furniture, such as sofas, or for floor-to-ceiling curtains, and add accents of bold colour or lavish texture through cushions, throws, blinds and bedspreads. This is the best way of stretching your budget and also makes it easy to ring the changes from winter to summer.

Left The natural linen of this sofa has been complemented by cushions of the same fabric, but with flaps in both vertical and horizontal arrangements. The cushion in the foreground is white linen with a taupe velvet band.
Opposite Black linen upholstery is offset by natural linen cushions banded to match the sofas. Other cushions in a stitched flower pattern add contrast. The sheer natural linen curtains pool generously on the floor.

CREATING A FABRIC BOARD

→ First choose the perfect linen to be the foundation of your scheme.

→ The tones of all the other fabrics that you select should relate to the undertone of that linen.

→ Fabric showrooms are often very mean with the size of free samples they provide, so it is worth purchasing bigger pieces in order to avoid expensive mistakes.

→ Decide what you would like each fabric to be used for and check that it is the correct weight for its intended purpose.

→ Lay out the fabrics so that they make sense in terms of how you are planning to use them. For example, if you have chosen one fabric for a pair of curtains and another for a curtain border, then lay them side by side.

→ Study the composition for a few days and make sure that you are happy with your selection.

→ Play with the fabric choices against other materials, such as carpet, wood stains and paint.

→ Put the fabric board alongside your original concept board and make sure that you have kept to your original vision in terms of mood and style.

Above Silver taupe wood (09) and a silk shag-pile carpet (15) create a luxurious foundation for this airy taupe scheme; a second option is given for darker taupe flooring (14). The sofas are in heavy linen (08) and linen damask (04), and are complemented by cushions in both matching damask and lighter weight natural linen (06 and 12). The armchairs are in textured taupe linen (05) with textured linen cushions in taupe and silver (07). Cushion bands are in a mix of natural linen (03) and dark taupe linen (11). An ottoman is upholstered in hair-on-hide (13). The Roman blind at the window is in silver linen (02) edged with a border of taupe velvet (10), complemented by sheer curtains in linen silk (01). The joinery is black oak (16).

Opposite This monochromatic scheme of black, white and grey for a master-bedroom suite has a core of white-lacquered joinery (07), grey long-pile silk carpet (09), and silver and grey linens of different weights and textures (04, 06 and 10). The headboard and TV unit are leather (05), with a woven finish for the furniture (08). Cotton Roman blinds (01) and sheer curtains (02) have been chosen for the windows. The bathroom features Scala blue stone (11) with a back-painted runner of glass (03).

Window Treatments

Unless you live in a very old and draughty house, the way you choose to dress your windows is decorative rather than practical. Your first consideration should be how much light you want to let in. For most of us, light is a life-enhancing feature and the more of it, the better. For this reason, you may well prefer sheers to heavy drapes, or louvred shutters to Roman blinds. However, there are other factors that may affect the sort of window treatment you choose, such as providing privacy from neighbours, the need for a blacked-out room for sleep, or for protecting antiques or artworks from light damage. Once you have resolved these practical questions, you can design beautiful window treatments accordingly.

Opposite Light can flood through this sheer linen curtain with its unobtrusive geometric pattern.

Left A dress-curtain pole with polished nickel fittings has been attached on each side of this French door, from which silvery taupe sheer curtains hang. The Roman blind over the door itself is made of dark taupe silk.

Curtains

Rather than choose curtain fabric simply for its colour or pattern, think also about how it feels and how it falls to the floor. Curtains are the evening gowns of the interior design world – they can be made in a host of glamorous and sensuous fabrics, so why opt for something pedestrian? Those that just touch the ground can look over-tailored, whereas soft fabric that pools on the floor creates a more opulent and luxurious feel. Cascades of voile, lace or unlined silk give privacy while allowing light to flood in unhindered.

Windows also provide an opportunity to underline the grid structure (see page 44) by bordering curtains in contrasting colours, both at the top and bottom. Pick up the accent colour of a border in other soft furnishings, such as cushions and bedspreads.

If you favour curtains over blinds, consider reflecting the seasons by having both under-curtains and a top set – the latter can be removed for the summer months, but will add a layer of warmth and cosiness during the winter. Remember that the most successful window treatments look as good at night when they are drawn as they do by day when open.

Poles and Finials

While it is possible to buy extremely elaborate and ornate curtain poles, they can detract from the whole effect if they are too dominant. On the whole, you do not want to draw attention to the fittings but to the furnishings, and the curtains should be one element of the entire scheme, rather than the focal point. Choose poles that complement the texture and colour of the drapes without overwhelming them. Curtain headings can be as simple as eyelets on a plain pole.

Paradoxically, it can be fun to choose finials that are more extrovert – being relatively small items, they will not dominate. Great finials work especially well if the ceilings are high. Finials also provide an opportunity to add another small layer of texture, such as bronze, glass or crystal, which can be echoed elsewhere in the scheme. Like door handles are to doors, think of finials as the jewellery of a very glamorous outfit.

WORKING WITH A CURTAIN MAKER

The way that curtains and blinds are made can make or break the entire look of a room. For this reason, you need to employ a professional maker who really understands the effect you want to create and knows exactly how to achieve it. Ask for references and to see examples of their previous work.

One of the first things you should discuss is how much 'dead space' to allow – this is the area of the wall both above and at the sides of the window that the curtains will cover. If you want to make a window look bigger, for example, you might extend the space outwards and cover some of the adjacent wall with curtain. If you want to make a window look taller, you can do so by adding a deep pelmet. The same applies to Roman blinds – how much either inside or outside of the reveal they are affects the whole look of the room.

You have to weigh up the advantages of improving a window's proportions against the drawback of losing some natural light. Once you have decided where precisely the curtains are to hang, your maker can take accurate dimensions. He or she will usually allow for at least twice as much fabric as the measurements suggest – two-and-a-half times for a really full and extravagant look.

You will also need to discuss the various options for lining and interlining. With an extra layer for insulation and thickness, interlined curtains give a heavier look, but if you want to achieve something softer and more ethereal, lined is better. It is worth noting that lined or interlined curtains last about twice as long as unlined ones, but the lining must be of a good quality, pre-shrunk and of a weight appropriate to that of your chosen fabric.

Headings should relate to the height of the curtains, so the taller the room, the deeper the heading should be.

Left Sheer curtains with a deep velvet border puddle to the dark-stained timber floor. Allow about 30cm (12in) of excess fabric in order to create this effect.

Above Cream fishnet curtains pool gracefully onto a stained oak floor.

This page *A taupe linen Roman blind, punctured with embroidered holes, has been double-lined to create a feeling of depth.*

Blinds

Available in an array of materials, including fabric, rattan, paper (as with Japanese shoji blinds) and wood, blinds generally best suit rooms that are clean and contemporary, in which they emphasize the architectural lines. They are also ideal as a way of imprinting symmetry and structure onto badly proportioned or awkwardly shaped windows.

Like curtains, fabric blinds can be made with contrasting runners of material to delineate the grid structure (see page 44). Ideal for providing privacy, their disadvantage is that they block out light – this is particularly true of Roman blinds, which cover at least half of the window even when open. Although blinds require less fabric than curtains, they are more complicated to make and fit, which can mean that the two level out in terms of cost.

Left A tone-on-tone Roman blind has been edged in the same pleated fabric as the curtains that hang over it.
Below The glossy lacquered finish of these deep-slatted shutters reflects light back into the room.

THE DOS AND DON'TS OF WINDOW TREATMENTS

→ Do think in terms of practicality: light, warmth, privacy and sleep.

→ Do choose fabric that is tactile as well as beautiful.

→ Do allow for seasonal changes.

→ Do consider whether you want runners or borders on curtains and blinds to emphasize the grid.

→ Do let fabric pool to the floor.

← Don't forget that window treatments can be designed specifically to improve proportions.

← Don't overlook the fact that blinds can look just as stunning as curtains.

← Don't blow the budget on over-elaborate curtain poles.

← Don't overlook the decorative possibilities of finials.

← Don't skimp on the making of curtains or blinds.

THE DOS AND DON'TS OF UPHOLSTERY

→ Do think about the sort of mood you wish the room to convey – fabrics help achieve this.

→ Do make up a fabric board and play with all the possibilities for upholstery and soft furnishings.

→ Do remember the importance of introducing contrasts of texture and weight.

→ Do choose fabric that suits the lines of the furniture.

→ Do keep to neutrals for big pieces of furniture.

← Don't be afraid to introduce some bold accents of colour, pattern or texture on smaller pieces.

← Don't forget to consider how the furniture will look from all angles.

← Don't ignore the potential of decorative stitching, trims and other finishes.

← Don't reject a very expensive fabric – a little can go a long way.

← Don't forget to protect fabric from stains and spills.

Upholstery

Far from being mundane, upholstery can transform furniture from bland to beautiful. It is not only the core fabric that counts, but also what you add in the way of trims or finishes.

Of course, there are matters of practicality to think about, particularly if you have young children or fur-shedding pets, but you can protect fabrics with Scotchgard or washable throws if need be. Check that your chosen fabric is fire-resistant – a professional upholsterer will not be allowed to work with fabric that has not been treated in this way.

Fabric Choices

Choosing a family of fabrics for a room is the ideal way to build up textural contrast within a scheme. This means not only selecting different types of fabric – such as linen, corduroy, tweed, velvet or suede – but varying the weights of fabric as well.

Make a fabric board (see page 150) and play with your choices, noting how they affect each other. You could also pin on the furniture shapes for which you are choosing materials – a clean-lined contemporary sofa, for example, may require a very different upholstery treatment from a vintage wing chair.

It is generally best to choose neutral shades for bigger pieces and then add a contrasting note of colour, texture or pattern on occasional chairs or stools. Treat these as accents within the room, just as you would a vase of flowers or a collection of glassware. The smaller the piece of furniture, the bolder you can go.

The other reason for choosing fabric in neutral colours for larger items of furniture is that upholstery is expensive, so you want a look that will date well – something comfortable and classic, rather than fashion led. Pay attention to the tactility of the fabric – when you come home after a long day, you want a sofa that you can sink into and enjoy for its comfort and feel as much as for its look.

Mood

Fabrics are also a way of imbuing a room with atmosphere, so think about what you are trying to achieve in the way of mood. A practical fabric such as denim, for example, denotes easy comfort and relaxation, but is not especially glamorous. Satin, on the other hand, is the mood opposite – a fabric that injects a note of high luxury even when used only as a trim.

While it is fun to play with fabrics of contrasting moods, the one you choose as the dominant ingredient will determine the overall feeling of the room. This is why linen is such a popular and intelligent choice – it is so versatile and various that it can be used universally, from country houses to city apartments, seaside cottages to ski chalets.

Detailing

A skilled upholsterer will guide you through the myriad ways of upholstering a single piece of furniture, with all the possible options for trimming, piping, nailing, stitching, skirting or buttoning. When deciding on upholstery, consider how a piece of furniture will be viewed from all angles – the backs of dining chairs, for example, can have as big an impact as their seating, while a boldly contrasting seat on an occasional chair can add just the right note of wit and energy. Remember, too, that if you fall in love with an expensive upholstery fabric that you cannot afford to use on a sofa, you could enjoy it as a trim for a sofa skirt or for covered buttons.

Cushions

So much more than an accessory to a bed, sofa or chair, cushions complete a scheme. In many ways they are miniature versions of the fabric board – an opportunity to be creative and imaginative with a variety of fabrics, trims and buttons. Because cushions are proportionately small in the room, they can take much bolder choices of colour or pattern. Their size, shape and tailoring will all influence the look and feel of a design.

Of course, a cushion should not be designed in isolation from the rest of the scheme. One of the reasons for creating a fabric board is to ensure that there are links between different areas of a room through its soft furnishings. If you add bands to the tops and bottoms of your curtains, for example, you could use the same fabric for the cushions. Similarly, if you upholster an occasional chair in a boldly contrasting texture to the sofa, you may decide to echo it subtly in one of the sofa cushions. In a room that has been designed around calm neutrals, one or two punchily coloured cushions can send different vibrations into a room.

The banding of cushions is another way of emphasizing the grid through strong vertical or horizontal lines (see page 44). Bands are easy to swap around, so if you choose plain linen cushion covers, you have the option to give them different looks according to the seasons, with banding in different textures and weights.

Runners and Throws

Like scaled-up versions of the banding on cushions, runners accentuate the lines of the room through contrasting texture or colour – whether used along the length of bedspreads or blinds, on the backs of chairs or down the centre of a table. They are also an excellent way to introduce seasonal change, being both easy and inexpensive to make.

Throws may have a practical purpose – to protect upholstery – or a purely decorative one. Organic and loose, they are particularly effective in a clean-lined room where they soften the hard edges. They also introduce a note of luxurious excess, particularly in combinations of fur, velvet, silk or cashmere. If you can't afford to re-upholster a sofa in a fabric you love, then invest in a couple of sumptuous throws instead.

KELLY'S TOP FIVE UPHOLSTERY FABRICS

01 Linen 02 Velvet 03 Suede 04 Leather 05 Chenille

KELLY'S TOP FIVE CUSHION STYLES

Folded over with one large button.

With a single or double contrasting band.

Linen overlaid with lace.

Plain in a single vibrant hue.

Both banded and buttoned.

This page Even the arms of this frame chair by Baltus are upholstered in white linen. The cushion is a darker linen with a velvet band.

Opposite A Baltus occasional chair with a black-lacquered ball frame is ideal in a room where it can be seen both from the back and front. The upholstery is silk embroidered in a geometric pattern.

ACCESSORIES

The way you accessorize a room is crucial to its overall composition and effect. Generally speaking, you will be in one of two camps: someone with artwork, treasured objects and decorative collections that need to be integrated into the scheme, or someone who is starting with a clean canvas and needs to decide how best to put the finishing touches to the room.

If you already have possessions that you want to include, then these need to be considered right at the start of the decorating process. Treat them as star pieces, which need a surface or wall on which to be displayed and which must be lit beautifully for maximum impact. However, just as you should try to avoid replicating an existing furniture layout, so you should try to cast a fresh eye on what you are displaying. A collection might have more impact if it is edited, focusing on playful changes of scale or textural contrast. Artwork and photographs may benefit from being remounted and reframed in harmony with the rest of the room. Objects that you usually group together may come to life if displayed differently.

Make sure that you leave space around objects. A room is often spoilt by too much treasured clutter, so be firm with yourself and remember: less is more. You don't have to throw away your mementoes – box them up and enjoy rediscovering them in a few years' time. Homes should not be static, so it makes sense to ring the changes with different accessories and art every now and then.

If you are looking for ways of styling a finished room from scratch, then you have the benefit of being able to buy exactly the shape and scale of objects needed for given areas, such as niches or floating shelves. Be imaginative: accessories need not cost a fortune. Even the simplest of objects can take on new relevance when replicated, be it a row of test-tube vases with a single bloom in each, or a montage of vintage black-and-white photographs. Avoid arrangements that are over-symmetrical to the point of dullness. Add in one or two things that create contrast, such as a vintage find or a hand-made craft object. As with furniture, do not be tempted to buy all your accessories from only one source – it is a quick and easy way to import a 'look', but it will lack personality.

Left Hand-made, black-lacquered resin jars contrast beautifully with sheer linen curtains.
Opposite This fabulous black-and-white Murano glass table lamp is complemented perfectly by a collection of silver-collared black glass vases.

The Art of Display

First, consider where you are planning to make a display. Open shelving is relatively inexpensive to build and can be made to your own dimensions and depth. Stained wood or clear glass are ideal choices for displaying books, or as a backdrop to an interesting collection that includes a variety of forms, colours or textures. You could also integrate discreet spotlighting into your display. 'Floating' shelves are easier to construct than you may think and are particularly effective in very contemporary interiors.

Building shelves into niches is an excellent way of making use of lost space. Niches are ideal for decorative collections of glassware, porcelain, silver or other rich textures. Choose a colour or finish for the backdrop that complements your display and think of it as a miniature theatre in which you are staging a performance for the eyes.

Freestanding cabinets with glazed, lockable doors are particularly suitable for valuable or fragile objects. Include some form of integrated lighting to show the collection off to its best advantage. Position display cabinets so that the eye is led towards them on entering a room.

Above Smooth taupe vases of varying sizes and shapes create an interesting display against the stone walls of a master bathroom, offset by antique silver-glass decanters.

Opposite top left An assortment of vintage glassware makes a pleasing tableau on a dining room console.

Opposite top right A sculptural Albedo table lamp by Lahumière Design complements a display of black-and-white photography.

Opposite bottom left A striking collection of crystal perfume bottles of different but complementary shapes denote glamour and luxury.

Opposite bottom right A group of textural vases and dishes plays against the matt surface of eggs in a glass bowl.

Opposite top left An ornate, distressed metal chandelier has sculptural impact when hung low over a circular mirror in a bedroom. A simple silver bowl of moss and succulents echoes the contours of the lacquered table from the Kelly Hoppen collection.

Opposite top right This white-lacquered coffee table, also by Kelly Hoppen, is recessed to accommodate an interesting table display – here a collection of plain cylindrical vases, each with a white rose head.

Opposite bottom left Ornate porcelain teapots, coloured glassware and a coral-on-plinth make an eclectic but successful display in a living room. The wall light in glass and steel is by Todhunter Earle.

Opposite bottom right A decorative heart in stone adds a textural note.

Above A collection of matt porcelain vessels in different shapes creates a pleasing still life in an entrance hall.

A mantelpiece is, in effect, a shelf over the fire. It has the advantage of being a natural focal point, so is ideal for displaying treasured objects, photographs or artworks. When dressing a mantelpiece, consider the impact of the display in terms of different scales and forms.

Table-top displays are ideal for objects best seen either from a bird's-eye view when standing, or at eye level when sitting. As with displays on a mantelpiece, the secret is to experiment with scale, form and texture until the right look is achieved. Shelves and tables gather dust, so make sure you maintain your display so that it always looks its best.

Artworks, such as paintings and photographs, do not have to be hung on walls – they can be propped up on shelves or mantelpieces to great effect. What matters is how well they are lit (see Accent Lighting, page 86) and that they are given space to 'breathe'. Valuable paintings should be protected from light damage, so do not place them in direct sunlight.

THE DOS AND DON'TS OF DISPLAY

→ Do remember that rooms can be transformed with the addition or removal of certain objects, so edit your possessions with this in mind.

→ Do think in terms of displaying clusters of objects, rather than individual ones.

→ Do leave space around the objects you display.

→ Do light your collections and artworks with care.

→ Do introduce a sense of symmetry, but break this up with a change of scale, texture or form.

← Don't forget to ring the changes regularly.

← Don't be careless with the things you display. A well-composed arrangement on a shelf or mantelpiece will quickly look cluttered if you add to it carelessly; a group of paintings will lose its impact if the pictures are not hung straight.

← Don't make a display that only works from one viewpoint; ensure that it looks good when seen from different points within the room.

← Don't overdo it – it is important to know when to stop.

← Don't throw things away when you tire of them – it is fun to rediscover objects after they have been stored away for a couple of years.

TOP 10 ACCESSORIES ON A BUDGET

01 Old paperback books tied into bundles.

02 Clear glass bowls filled with moss, white sand and sustainable coral.

03 Piles of blue-and-white vintage plates.

04 One-colour glass from flea markets and antique shops.

05 Black-and-white photographs.

06 Test-tube vases with single stems.

07 A medley of mirrors or empty frames.

08 Kitchen trays filled with gourds.

09 High-street-bought ceramic vessels in white or cream.

10 Multiples of anything.

Right A row of 'Norma Jean' cream roses makes the centrepiece to a dining table – displayed here in gold bubble fishbowl vases and flower vases with a triple-spiked base.

Opposite top left A soft palette of nude roses displayed in ceramic vases with a pearlized lustre.

Opposite top right Floating rose heads in a large clear glass vase look magical.

Above Green hydrangea heads, cut very short, are displayed here in silver-rimmed glass vases.

Right Large, shallow, nickel bowls are filled with green moss and echeveria.

Below right Green hydrangea stems look striking displayed in a row of floor-standing, cylindrical, black glass vases.

Below Clear cylindrial glasses with a moss ball in each are displayed on Kelly Hoppen tables.

Opposite bottom A simple vase of white hydrangea heads add the finishing touch to a bathroom.

Mood Enhancement

It is not just how a home looks that matters, but how it feels when you walk into it. The principles behind feng shui are based on the idea that positive energy should be able to circulate freely. If that energy becomes blocked, the whole atmosphere of a room can change for the worse. To understand this, you have to accept that everything is made of energy – including us. Energy is circulating through your home the entire time, even if you cannot see it. Crystals, candles, wind chimes, mirrors, plants and music can all be used to unblock energy – a sort of acupuncture for the home.

The fact is that many feng shui principles – or other equivalents, such as Japanese *kaso* or Indian *vaastu shastra* – come down to common sense. Energy is blocked by objects being in the wrong place, so make sure you tidy up, and make it easy to do so by having adequate storage. Don't accumulate clutter – old paper, never-worn clothes or things you haven't used for a couple of years should either be boxed up out of sight or disposed of entirely. In fact, many feng shui consultants believe that if you eliminate clutter from your life, 80 per cent of the energy-improving work is done.

Mood is also about adding a final layer of sensuality to your home. Scent is one of the most evocative and powerful instruments at our disposal, so if you have a favourite scented candle, then buy it by the dozen and light it every time you step through the door. It is an instant remedy for the stresses of the day. Fresh flowers are also guaranteed pick-me-ups – don't view them as an occasional luxury but as one of the must-haves of life. Even a few stems can go a long way in terms of mood enhancement.

Candles and dimmed lighting are far more soothing than bright artificial light can ever be. And music that you love will also promote good energy. Come on: be kind to yourself. Once you have created your dream home, you deserve these final ingredients in order to enjoy it to the full.

Below left Consider how even the simplest of objects is displayed. These white ceramic bowls are shrouded by chainmail.

Below The addition of flowers is one of the easiest ways to make a room feel refreshed and loved.

Opposite Mirrors are not only ornamental but can bounce positive energy around a space.

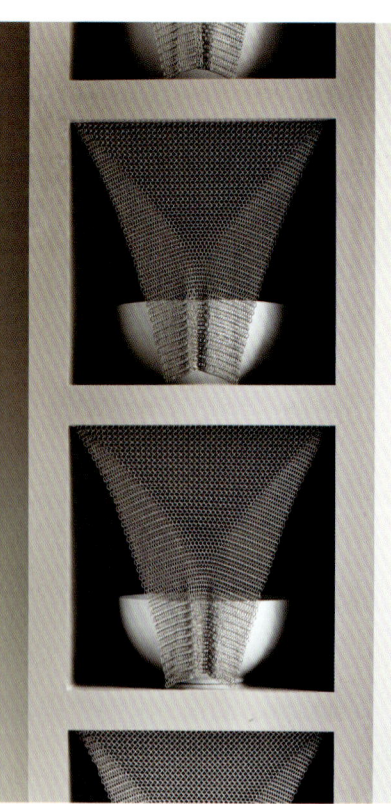

DESIGNING ROOMS

CREATING A GOOD IMPRESSION
THE CORE OF THE HOME

If you are designing an entire house, begin with the hall. The reason for this is that the hall and the stairs are the core of the home around which all else revolves. Not only is the hall the first area that people see – making a powerful first impression – but it is also glimpsed from every other principal room into which it leads. The hall must set the style signature of the home. Get this right and all else will follow.

The staircase is equally important. At one time, it was almost unheard of for people to rip out existing staircases, at best giving them a new lick of paint, but those days are gone. Unless you are fortunate enough to have inherited a beautiful architectural statement or a period (and possibly protected) design, then you should assess your staircase as you would any other feature. It is truly incredible how much of a difference it can make to begin with a fresh eye on the biggest design statement within a house, rather than trying to 'make do and mend'.

The Front Door

It is essential to choose or commission a front door that sets the seal on the house, architecturally and stylistically. It needs to be in proportion with the rest of the building, but that does not mean it cannot be bigger than is usual. Just as internal doors may be scaled up to give them more presence, so front doors can often be heightened and broadened to good effect. Choose fittings in keeping with the overall design. Porches are a practical addition, but they must also be conceived as part of the whole look.

A front door has to look as good from the inside as it does from the outside. It needs to offer a sense of security and protection on the one hand, and be welcoming on the other. If you cannot find the sort of door you envisage, hire an interior architect to help you bring your ideas to fruition. You will be astounded by the choice of materials, finishes and fittings on offer. Never compromise on the front door: it is the signature element of your home.

Opposite The front door is the first indication of the home beyond. This bespoke contemporary panelled door has been commissioned from oak, stained dark oyster. Its imposing height, breadth and thickness add to the sense of having arrived at a memorable destination.

Entrance Halls

Do not design the hall in isolation. Because it sets the seal on the look of the house as a whole, it needs to send visual reverberations throughout. Lay the design board for the hall alongside those of adjacent rooms, so that you can pick up a sense of how they will complement each other in terms of colours, textures and finishes.

Think, first of all, about what the eye will see when you walk in. What is the focal point? When it comes to design and decoration, allow yourself to push the boat out in terms of budget. Halls are not generally the largest areas of the house, so you can afford to do something special with them, whether it is a luxurious wall finish, a spectacular piece of furniture or a statement light. The design of the hall is not so much about impressing visitors as making yourself feel happy from the moment you step through the front door.

Remember the practical considerations, too: a place to hang coats, leave wet umbrellas, put down keys or store the pushchair. Make a list of all the requirements of your hall and ensure you resolve them fully.

Use the grid (see page 44) to reinforce a strong sense of design. Creating runners on the floor by contrasting stones or timbers, or a mix of both, is an ideal way of signposting the eye towards the principal rooms. Doors emphasize the vertical planes, so balance these with horizontal lines, such as console tables or extra-deep skirting boards.

Above left A convex mirror of black and gold gives an unusual view of this handsome staircase, constructed from oak and iron. The mirror also helps to bounce light back into the room.

Centre left The view down the length of an entrance lobby, where the slatted dark timber walls have been lit between the grooves, to dramatic effect. A polished marble runner inset into the dark timber floor leads the eye forwards.

Below left The hall is also the perfect place in which to display treasured paintings and other objects. Here a fine oil painting is hung over a contemporary scagliola console table.

Opposite This gracefully sweeping staircase of timber and glass is the key architectural feature in this elegant London townhouse. The chainmail light by Terzani is hung purposefully off-centre, making a play of texture and scale. The circular lacquered table, on which are displayed richly textured vessels, harmonizes perfectly with the low leather bench.

Stairs

The staircase underpins the house both physically and aesthetically. Custom-designed examples take a house to new heights, literally and stylistically. However, if you are thinking of replacing an existing staircase, you must seek the help of an architect (see page 268), because the engineering involved is highly complex. An architect will also be able to advise on the many choices bespoke staircases offer, from the curving 'whipped cream' effect to the magic of 'floating' treads, apparently hanging in thin air. Be warned, though: staircases do not come cheap, given the high level of skill and time involved in their creation.

There are ways of rejuvenating existing staircases that are also effective. You could, for example, commission new banisters or handrails – or box in the finials for a more contemporary look. If the treads and risers are deep enough, it may be possible to re-clad them in stone, but a simpler solution would be to re-stain the wood to a shade more in keeping with the rest of your home.

Fitted carpet on stairs tends to look dated – it is better to use runners of carpet with contrast edging against stained or painted timber stairs. Not only does it look wonderfully elegant, but it is also quiet and comfortable underfoot.

Right A fabulous spiralling crystal chandelier by Spina cascades dramatically down two levels through the centre of the stairwell. Its tip can be seen in the image of the hall on the bottom left of the previous spread.

Above left Consider the vista from one room to the next. Here, the geometrically carved doors open in one continuous line.

Above This is the opposite view of that shown on page 177, illustrating the importance of the front door both when looking in and looking out. Note how the lobby lights cast interesting reflections onto the polished stone floor.

Left Shadow-gap lighting makes staircases safer and brings out the texture of materials, such as this silk-viscose carpet.

Opposite top left A different view of the Gaudí-like staircase shown on page 179. Its organic shape plays perfectly against the clean architectural lines of the double-height windows. The panels of glass make it appear lighter and more fluid.

Opposite top right A view down the same staircase shows how it has been moulded to create a galleried effect on the floor above. Taupe wool stair carpet has been edged with a darker taupe, emphasizing the contours.

Circulation and Flow

It does not make sense to consider halls separately from stairs, corridors and other connected areas. You may not want to decorate all of these in exactly the same way, but there should be a visual thread that connects them together. The use of a neutral palette (see page 104) makes this easy to do, as it creates a base foundation of colour to which other textures and accents can be added with ease.

Think about how each room leads into the next and what can be seen from the hall looking in, or vice versa. Ground-floor cloakrooms, for example, are more likely to link to the design of the hall than to other bathrooms within the house, and for that reason, they can be styled with more panache (see page 256).

Remember, too, the importance of vertical views within the hall and up the staircase. Encourage the eye to sweep upwards by hanging a magnificent light in the stairwell, or by positioning tall mirrors in such a way that they emphasize height. The hall is the beginning of the journey throughout the house and should engender a feeling of warm anticipation.

Lighting

The lighting of the hall and stairs needs to combine the same regard for general, task and mood lighting as other areas (see pages 84–91). The most essential consideration, however, is ease of use. Unless you have a pre-programmed lighting system, you must ensure that you can switch on the hall light the moment you step through the front door – and that you can control it from other levels. Stairs also need good lighting. Shadow-gap lighting at the side of stair treads is both beautifully atmospheric and a safety feature, providing a low-level glow that can be left on all night. Floor washers set into the perimeters of hall floors are also an effective choice.

Stairwell lighting is often the star piece of the hall, such as a dramatically over-scaled statement chandelier that cascades down several levels. Often such pieces are not designed to be efficient light sources themselves, but are illuminated by spotlights positioned to wash light down the walls and stairs. Accent lighting can be used to show any artwork or *objets* to best advantage.

DESIGNING THE HALL AND STAIRS

→ When designing your house, begin with the hall because it sets the tone throughout.

→ Lay the design boards for adjoining rooms side by side, so that you can see the complete look.

→ Resolve practical considerations, such as where to hang coats.

→ Think about circulation and flow from the hall to other adjoining areas.

→ Consider whether the staircase could be replaced or revitalized.

→ Set aside some of the budget for a customized front door.

→ Make sure lighting is both safe and mood-enhancing.

→ Always contrive a 'Wow!' moment for when you walk through the front door.

Opposite This sweeping staircase is complemented by bespoke feature pendants, suspended through three floors and anchored to a skylight above. The underside of the staircase is lit with mini LED uplighters, creating indirect light that bounces back onto the stone floor.

Above Shadow-gap lighting has been created by mounting a simple profile onto the skirting that conceals a warm LED strip. This gives a soft wash of light that guides the eye down the corridor. Eastern-style feature pendants of glass and metal add character.

GATHER TOGETHER
LIVING ROOMS

More than any other room, the living room demands careful thought about how it is going to be used, by whom and at what time of day. The living room is as likely to be a family snug adjoining the kitchen – now, for many, the nerve centre of the house – as a separate, enclosed room. Formal living rooms are increasingly used only when entertaining and, like any semi-redundant space, there is a danger of them feeling rather cold and uncomfortable.

The success of a living room lies in it being used on a regular basis. Encourage family and friends to make themselves as comfortable as possible here, with inviting sofas, subtle lighting, a quality audio-visual (AV) system and your favourite scented candles. Even if you entertain in the kitchen more than the dining room, invite guests to gravitate towards the living room for after-dinner conversation and downtime. A room that is loved and used will pay dividends in ways that a largely ignored one never can.

Left and below *Two views of the same lavishly decorated living room. The sofas and armchairs are upholstered in black linen, contrasting with the natural-coloured linen of the ottoman. The mirror-topped tables are from the Kelly Hoppen range, while the brass lights are by Ochre. The low fireplace, against a textured plaster wall, can be viewed from the adjacent hall (see pages 26–7).*

Key Considerations

The first and most obvious question is whether you want to have a television in the living room and, if so, where it will go. The fact is that television is a feature of most of our lives, even if we only watch it for the news or an occasional film. Modern AV systems offer an extensive menu of choice, from concealed wall-mounted screens to pop-up cabinetry versions. You don't have to conceal the television, but what matters is to design the layout (see page 190) in such a way that the eye is drawn to other zones within the room, not just to the screen.

The second question is whether there is a fireplace and, if so, is it to be used? (Check chimneys and flue linings before doing so.) There are many contemporary and 'green' alternatives to traditional open fires that still give the same sense of comfort and warmth without burning solid fuel. These are not necessarily the same height and width as traditional fireplaces – they are as likely to be low and rectangular as tall and square. As a key focal point within the room, the fireplace is one of the first things to be decided before designing the rest of the scheme. A cleverly thought-out fireplace can also be used to give a sense of symmetry and balance to a room that is architecturally lacking in both.

Finally, give careful thought as to how multi-functional this space needs to be. Does it have to cater for very young children? For pre-teens or teens (and, of course, their friends)? Will you allow your dogs on the sofa or let your cats claw at the curtains? In other words, how precious do you intend to be about furniture and furnishings? It may be that you should allow for muddy trainers, spilled drinks or grubby fingers and choose finishes and fabrics accordingly. Analysing the function of a room – what and who – will also indicate how much storage you need, where lighting is best positioned and how to zone the room effectively.

Right There is nothing more inviting than a fire around which to gather. This sleek, contemporary design blends perfectly into the media wall, echoing the lines of the shelf below. Other key pieces include the bronze light with LED tubes by Roll and Hill and the floating glass cabinets for display.

Layout

Designing the layout of a living room is all about zoning (see page 41). Unless you have a very small living space, you should try to have two or even three sitting areas. One of these is likely to be for comfortable watching of the television, but you may have another group of sofas or chairs set away from this, perhaps in front of the fire. You don't need a physical screen between one zone and the other, but you may suggest invisible boundaries in the way that furniture faces, say, or by punctuating the line of vision with a pair of lamps or a well-placed console table. Remember the importance of the grid (see page 44). This will help you decide how best to demarcate the different areas of the house, emphasizing the design through the interplay of vertical and horizontal lines.

The only way to design multi-functional spaces effectively is by drawing up a floor plan and working out which pieces of furniture should go where (see page 57). The layout is all-important because this determines where lighting needs to go, which in turn is essential for wiring the room correctly. If you are having floor-mounted sockets for lamps, for example, it is absolutely crucial that you do not change your mind regarding their position once the wood or carpet has been cut into in order to fit them.

Allow breathing space around furniture, art and objects – a good layout is not about cramming as much as possible into a room. Remember the importance of flow (see page 42) – that sense of easy comfort that makes a room look inviting and engenders a feeling of well-being when moving around it.

Think about practicalities, too. Every chair or sofa should have a surface close at hand on which a visitor could rest a cup or a glass. Sofas should not be so high that people perch on the edge, nor so deep that they risk backache from lack of support. Lamps should be adjustable in height for reading. Storage is also a major requirement: whether fitted or freestanding, it should be custom-made for your needs, providing a clutter-free solution for this multi-purpose space.

Try to avoid repeating the previous layout from sheer habit. One of the quickest ways of refreshing a room is to completely rethink the furniture layout along with the decoration. If you have one or two pieces of furniture whose size alone determines where everything else can go, you should think about sending them to a saleroom or putting them into storage and freeing yourself from those constraints.

Finally, do remember that a zone is not necessarily about furniture. If, perhaps, you have a particularly fine artwork that you wish people to notice, you should put it at the centre of its own zone, with everything else arranged to lead the eye towards it.

IN DETAIL
LIVING ROOM LAYOUT

Design an extra-large living room with thought and care for a successful result.

01 Decide how many zones you need within the room – there are four here.

02 Mark out the seating areas accordingly.

03 Position tables and lamps to correspond with the seating.

04 Allow sufficient space for easy flow around furniture.

05 Use sculptural pieces, such as a day bed, as punctuation points within the space.

06 Make sure that all lamps are close to power points.

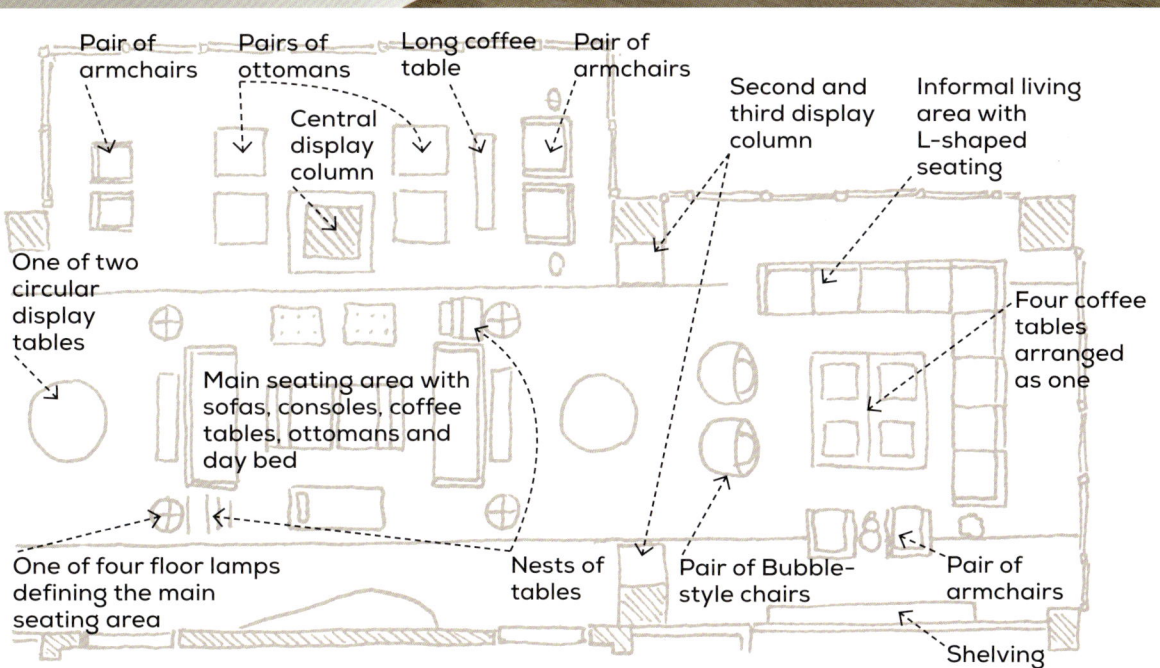

Above Harmony has been achieved in this triple-aspect drawing room by creating symmetry and balance. Central to the room are two main seating areas, one with a pair of sofas placed opposite each other, and an L-shaped configuration offset by two Bubble-style chairs. Additional seating areas by the windows are more intimate and semi-private.

Right A continuation of the plan seen on page 68 shows the seating area on the right with an informal arrangement of L-shaped modular furniture and Bubble-style chairs. Four coffee tables put together suit the scale of the room. Two smaller display columns mark the divide between the formal and informal.

Style

The way you zone a room – for example, by arranging furniture in a way that is formal or informal – is a major indicator of its style. Is this a room to be used predominantly for formal entertaining or as a place for the family to chill out? Must it have both a public and a private face? Does it function differently by day and by night? The way you answer these questions is crucial when it comes to deciding on the look of your living space.

You should also think about how the living area links visually to adjacent rooms, most particularly the hall or the dining room. Having a good sense of flow through the house means the senses should not jar between one room and the next. There should be a feeling of harmony and balance. Consider internal vistas, both those as you enter the room and the glimpses of other rooms you see from within it.

One of the major advantages of working with a neutral palette (see page 104) is that the big planes of the room – walls and floors, in particular – become a clean, calm canvas to which additional tones and textures can be introduced. Living rooms are often the place where good pieces of art are hung, so you need a wall colour or finish that does not fight with these, but instead displays them to good advantage.

Floors must be both practical and comfortable underfoot, but you can accentuate zoned areas through a change of surface or the addition of rugs. Double-glazed windows need very little in the way of curtains for reasons of insulation, but window treatments offer a way of combining simplicity of style with paradoxically glamorous and sensual fabrics.

When designing your fabric and furnishings board, remember that every living room should have its star piece, whether that is a striking item of furniture, a lavish fabric or a sculpture. Keep this at the forefront of your mind, and choose textures and colours that will show it off to the full. Big pieces of furniture, such as sofas, can dominate too much if upholstered in bright or bold fabric. It is better to keep them textured and neutral and to introduce accents of interest with cushions, throws or the coverings of small, occasional chairs.

LIVING ROOM TICK LIST

- Make a list of all the functions this room has to deliver for the various people who use it.
- Consider how the space can be zoned accordingly.
- Decide where the television will go and whether to conceal or display it.
- Draw a plan showing any permanent fixtures, such as fireplaces and cabinetry.
- Use this to determine a layout that allows for the zoning you want.
- Design a lighting scheme that reflects this layout.
- Ensure you have allowed for sufficient storage.
- Choose a furnishing scheme that is both practical and pleasing in terms of the many functions of the room.
- Incorporate at least one star piece that creates a 'Wow!' moment.
- Spend time arranging displays of pictures or objects that enhance the whole look.

Opposite top This intimate family space has been designed around a colour scheme of blues and greens. While blue is often considered a cold colour, these ocean shades imbue the atmosphere with comfort. In the fireplace is a fire sculpture by BD Designs. To the right is an iconic Eames Lounge chair and ottoman.

Opposite bottom left and right The luxuriously deep pile of this shaggy silk carpet makes this warm-toned living space welcoming and comfortable. The deep reds of the velvet cushion banding and the charcoal plaster finish of the media wall emphasize this richly layered mood.

Lighting

The lighting in a living room must be designed to work around the layout of the furniture. Whether you need lights for reading, playing cards or an activity such as knitting, this must be decided at the very beginning so that power points can be positioned accordingly.

It is likely that you will need three or four separate lighting circuits to give a good mix of general, task and mood light (see pages 80–95). These will need to be installed before the flooring is laid or any decoration begins. Overhead general lights are never flattering because they diffuse light across the room, making everything seem flat and dull. You may want to hang one as a statement piece, but you will achieve better results if you enhance the illumination with downlighters or uplighters – or a combination – at the sides of the room, which will wash the walls and furniture with light and 'bounce' it back into the room. The living room is also the ideal place in which to incorporate a 5-amp circuit, which allows you to operate a number of lamps with one control and dim them when appropriate.

Remember that lighting should be layered so as to offer as much versatility as possible. In a living room, it may be as important to boost low winter daylight as to design a scheme that is comfortable and inviting at night. Special features, such as artworks, should be enhanced with well-controlled directional light – the tighter the beam, the more directional the light. Reading lamps should be adjusted to the correct height, so that you do not read in your own shadow.

Even the subtlest additions to a lighting scheme can make an incredible difference to the feel of a room. If you are having floating shelves or other cabinetry installed, commission integrated lighting that highlights the objects on display when you dim the general lighting. Alternatively, ask for architectural lighting tubes to be laid on the top of bookcases, so that they will wash the walls above with a soft glow. Picture rails offer the ideal place for LED strips to be fixed to uplight period cornices to fabulous effect. Don't under-estimate the importance of candles – they might not cast much illumination, but as an additional layer of mood lighting they are both effective and relatively inexpensive.

CGI: LIVING ROOM LIGHTING

In addition to re-creating a design in terms of furniture layouts, texture and colour, CGIs can be used to see the effect of suggested lighting within a room. In this living room, for example, the image shows not only the recessed spots that provide general light, but also the pools of shadow and light they make on different surfaces. The shelves have been under-lit to accentuate their 'floating' appearance, proving how effective this would be in reality. A sculptural lamp has been positioned on each side of the room for directional light – ideal for reading or working on the laptop. The central chandelier is a star piece within the room, exuberantly at odds with the clean lines around it, and hung relatively low over the coffee table for even greater impact. Even the fire contributes to the ambient background glow.

Above Indirect cove lights create a warm glow that is particularly pleasing after dark. The way that the light bounces off the reflective ceiling of the yacht gives an illusion of further height in a restrictive space. The feature fitting over the coffee table is dimmed in the evening to add to the feeling of cosiness and comfort.

Right Five simple pendant lights have been chosen instead of one single fitting to illuminate this richly toned seating area. The pool of light they jointly create adds atmosphere.

Display

The living room is often the place where art, collections or treasured objects are displayed. These should be integrated into your scheme from the start, as part of the zoning of the room. It may be that you will commission shelves or cabinetry for display, or that you have the perfect freestanding piece. The art and other objects that you want to display are central to the decisions you make about lighting – whether you choose to have it integrated into furniture and in terms of how you position directional spotlights.

A group of paintings or a collection of objects is often enhanced by some skilful editing. That is why collectors often rotate their possessions, rather than trying to show everything at once.

With paintings, you often need to physically move them around until you find the perfect position. The key consideration is whether you want to highlight an individual work or create a group impact. If the former, make sure nothing else close by fights for attention. If the latter, think about having the paintings framed and mounted in a similar style, to visually unite them. Do not hang them too high – paintings should be at eye level, not top-of-head height.

Collections also need a sense of space. A group of similar objects has great visual impact, but too many look cluttered. Be disciplined and choose the best items in your collection to display instead of squeezing everything in.

When it comes to concocting an interesting display of disparate objects, decide on a centrepiece and radiate out from this. Don't be too symmetrical or uniform, but instead concentrate on how each object can balance another. The secret is to avoid a confusing mishmash by finding themes that can be echoed throughout. Creating a display is a small-scale version of designing a room: it still comes down to understanding form, scale, texture and colour.

Below left A collection of vases, bowls, books and objets *is displayed on floor-to-ceiling wooden shelves.*

Below centre A detail of the Mondrian dresser designed by Kelly Hoppen for Smallbone. Black textured wood and black lacquer make a dramatic backdrop for creamy vases of peonies.

Below right Bespoke glass cabinets with integral lighting are the ideal place in which to preserve and display rare antiquarian books.

Opposite A custom-built storage column, lacquered in white with chrome-edged niches, provides an unusual display setting for a collection of glassware.

KEY PIECES

Statement chairs, opposite top left A Makasar ebony Aspre lounge chair by Christian Liaigre, upholstered in white leather, takes pride of place in a luxuriously layered room.

Star piece, opposite top right A design classic, such as this contemporary interpretation of the iconic Bubble chair, will work with many different styles of furniture and décor. Here its curved shape is juxtaposed with the rigid lines of square coffee tables and modular seating.

Comfortable sofas, opposite below Inviting, generously proportioned seating is a key feature of any living space. Here a pair of Massant armchairs upholstered in black leather has been partnered with a deep sofa upholstered in charcoal waxed linen. A mix of table styles in wood, metal and glass play against the intrinsic symmetry of the room. The lamps are by Heathfield.

Coffee table, below A coffee table, as large as your living space will comfortably allow, provides an additional surface for display as well as being practical. This mirror-topped, square, lacquered coffee table is from the Kelly Hoppen collection.

Occasional tables, right, top to bottom Providing a convenient surface within reach of all the seating, occasional tables can also be used for displaying objects, table lamps or flowers and add another layer of texture to a scheme. These timber side tables with rivet detail are from the Kelly Hoppen collection. A nest of dark walnut hand-crafted tables creates unusual shadows on the floor. A sleek, sculptural white-lacquered side table by Sé adds an organic twist to the linear style of the other furniture. The vintage-style side table with inlaid mirrored top is also from the Kelly Hoppen collection.

Home Studies

The rooms in which we work at home are less like conventional offices and more akin to old-fashioned studies. They are library-style spaces that centre on peace, tranquillity and contemplation. With advancements in wireless technology, it is no longer necessary to have a jungle of unsightly cables on the study floor. Instead, the focus is on the furniture, fabrics and artworks that imbue the space with personality and wit.

The desk is the star of the room and, as such, it should be placed centrally rather than against one wall. There are many wonderful designs, so choose one that is comfortable to sit at, practical for your needs and also looks striking. Choose a chair that complements it beautifully – not necessarily an 'office' design, but perhaps a vintage wing chair or a sculptural piece of contemporary design. Think how you could zone the room by creating another seating area for reading, with a low armchair, lamp and side table. Don't choose two chairs of the same design – introduce some contrast through form, texture or colour.

Design customized and integrated storage that fits all your needs, including a place to keep the printer. Ideally, this could be concealed behind attractive joinery, rather than allowing paper and equipment to clutter the room. Floating shelves should be included, both for books and for displaying photographs, trophies or other mementoes – a study is a very personal space.

Studies are often small rooms and ideal for using the grid to create symmetry and proportion. This could be through a runner of contrasting flooring leading into the room, or a runner taking the eye up the far wall.

A study should feel different from the rest of the house, being designed with just one person in mind, but it must also connect visually to the hall and adjacent rooms.

Opposite This glass-topped table on black-lacquered legs by Baltus is the centrepiece of this elegantly simple office. Murano glass pendants in opal, pearl and smoky grey have been used to construct an unusual light – they also give the eye something to contemplate when taking a break from the computer screen.

Above left Good lighting is a must for reading and working. This Kevin Reilly card pendant hovering over the table casts a comfortable glow and adds a note of distinction.

Above right An architectural glass-topped desk, with black-lacquered trestle-style legs, is positioned in front of over-sized shelving with a display of moss-filled fishbowls. The two-headed metal lamp is by Ochre.

COOK AND CHAT KITCHENS

A kitchen may look simple, but it is the most complicated room to design, because everything is working 'behind the scenes'. It is not enough to create one that looks stunning – you have to consider where every item will go, from the largest appliance to the smallest teaspoon. You also need to be honest about how much cooking you will do. There is nothing more maddening than working in a kitchen that is cluttered with equipment that nobody uses.

The kitchen today is about more than cooking. It is the place where friends and family gather to chat and where people often choose to entertain informally, so it may well include a snug area with an AV system and cosy seating. The kitchen has become a multi-functional, multi-layered room – a hybrid between cooking, eating and living.

Style

Visit as many showrooms as possible before you decide on whom to appoint to fit your kitchen and don't make rushed decisions. It is no wonder that most kitchens cost double the initial quote when you take into account appliances, floors, lighting, decorative finishes and accessories.

Even if you are working with a kitchen designer, make a concept board that shows images and materials you like, whether it is particular stones or timbers, finishes such as coloured glass or lacquer, or designs of door handles. This will concentrate your chosen designer's mind on creating a kitchen that really is right for you. Begin to think of ways of introducing textural contrast – polished plaster with lacquer, say, or concrete with glass – and consider how you might use different materials to mark out zones.

There are some items on which it is worth spending more money to have something truly special. Kitchen taps are akin to pieces of sculpture, so push the boat out when deciding on these. The door furniture probably sets the tone of the kitchen more than any other item, so choose something that is beautiful, tactile and efficiently designed.

Right This fabulously streamlined Poggenpohl kitchen features a floor and worktops in different-coloured quartz, and units in teak and resin. The elegant sculptural taps are by Dornbracht. The bar stools have been upholstered in taupe leather to complement the rest of the scheme. Task lighting is provided by simple glass pendants hanging in a row above this island unit (one of two).

This page The kitchen bar of the Kelly Hoppen kitchen for Smallbone features white marble cutting through white textured wood. The open storage unit is of pure taupe lacquer with chainmail detailing.

Opposite The Kelly Hoppen range for Smallbone features a pure white circular island with drop-level hob and cantilevered seating area.

Key Considerations

The way you approach the design of a kitchen will vary hugely according to whether you are replacing an existing one or relocating it to a different room within the house. We spend a lot of time in our kitchens – they really have become the beating heart of the home – so it makes sense to position yours in a room with a good aspect and lots of natural light. In recent years, there has been a vogue to site kitchens in extended basement areas, but these tend to be low, dark rooms that rely heavily on artificial light. It may be preferable to use one of the better-proportioned rooms on the floor above and enjoy spending time in a space with high ceilings, big windows and an airy atmosphere. Of course, it will cost more to relocate a kitchen, rather than replicate an existing one, but this is a room you must get right in order to live happily in your home. Kitchens are costly and installing one causes maximum disruption, so you want to achieve the best result you can.

Think, too, about how the kitchen connects to other rooms and to outside spaces. The idea of flow (see page 42) is very important, particularly when it comes to practical issues, such as taking food to the dining room or to the garden. If you are starting from scratch with the design of your house, work with your architect to find the optimum location for the kitchen – in effect, all the other rooms should radiate off from this point.

If you are re-siting a kitchen, you need to understand the limitations that you might face. Take advice, for instance, on where the extractor can be positioned, as this will determine where the hob will be. If the hob is to be on an island unit, it may be necessary to have an artificial ceiling built for ducting and extraction. The oven and hob should be within easy access of the sink and fridge. However, the fridge is likely to be one of the largest objects in the room, so you will probably want it to be tucked discreetly into a corner, rather than taking centre stage. In other words, a kitchen is a jigsaw puzzle that needs careful solving.

Most kitchens lend themselves to certain layouts, and a kitchen specialist is the best person to advise, but it is also worth asking your builder, plumber and electrician whether there are constraints of which you need to be aware.

Layout

A good kitchen designer will come up with a solution that will surpass your expectations. Where they show their expertise is often in the ingenious storage solutions they suggest, particularly for unwieldy but essential items, such as food processors or microwave ovens. However, treat some of their suggestions with a degree of cynicism. It is very much in their interests to sell you as many additional items as possible, but are you sure you really want a tap for instant boiling water, a teriyaki grill or an integrated wine cooler? Gadgets come in and out of fashion and few are worth the extra money. Remember, too, that cupboards with drawers cost more than those without, so go through the price breakdown carefully to see where money might be saved. Stay grounded. You don't want to end up with an entire wall of expensive appliances and not enough storage or work surfaces, so be careful not to be carried away with your kitchen designer's enthusiasm.

Functionality

Consider how you and your family will use this space (see page 14). Go back to the idea of zoning (see page 41), by writing a list of all that has to be done within the kitchen and deciding where best these activities might take place within the space available. Remember, each zone will have to be lit well, according to its use.

Imagine all the tasks you will be doing in the kitchen and visualize how they will work in reality. For example, a dishwasher needs space around it for stacking dirty plates and unloading clean ones; a sink needs an adequate draining area; an oven needs an adjoining surface on which to stand hot dishes. This might sound obvious, but it is surprising how many people agree to a kitchen layout that does not fulfil practical requirements. Decide what you would like to display and what you would prefer to keep hidden, and ensure you have adequate means to accommodate both.

Functionality is all. Do not become so fixated on a particular layout or style that you can't be objective about its advantages and disadvantages. The worst kitchens are those on which someone has spent a fortune and yet there is no clear place for the kettle or toaster. Island units are a menace rather than a benefit if you seem to spend your entire time running laps around one when cooking.

Consider maintenance, too. Some work surfaces, such as stone, can be a headache if you spill red wine or oil; wood often marks with repeated subjection to water – so man-made composites are often preferable. Floors have to be able to withstand water, spillages and the scraping of chair legs. Sinks must be as stain-resistant as possible.

QUESTIONNAIRE: KITCHEN FUNCTIONALITY

→ Would you like a breakfast bar or a table to eat at?

→ Is there room for a separate utility area?

→ Do you need space for pets?

→ Should there be a quiet corner for homework or a place to use the laptop?

→ Do you need to cater for messy craft or art activities?

→ What kind of dishes do you cook most and do you need special equipment? Where will you site it and does it require a power point?

→ How tall are you?

→ Are there safety concerns (if you have young children, for example)?

→ If you entertain here, where will guests sit while you cook?

→ Do you want an AV system? Air-conditioning?

Above left On a yacht, white-lacquered units with a black quartz worktop create a bold statement. The taupe-coloured timber floor unites this area with the rest of the deck.

Opposite top A Boffi black-lacquered kitchen with a stone composite work surface is complemented by specialist plaster walls and lacquered shutters. The central island creates a galley effect.

Opposite below The key materials of the Kelly Hoppen kitchen for Smallbone are taupe and white textured wood, glass, marble, and taupe and white lacquer. The chrome stools are upholstered in white leather.

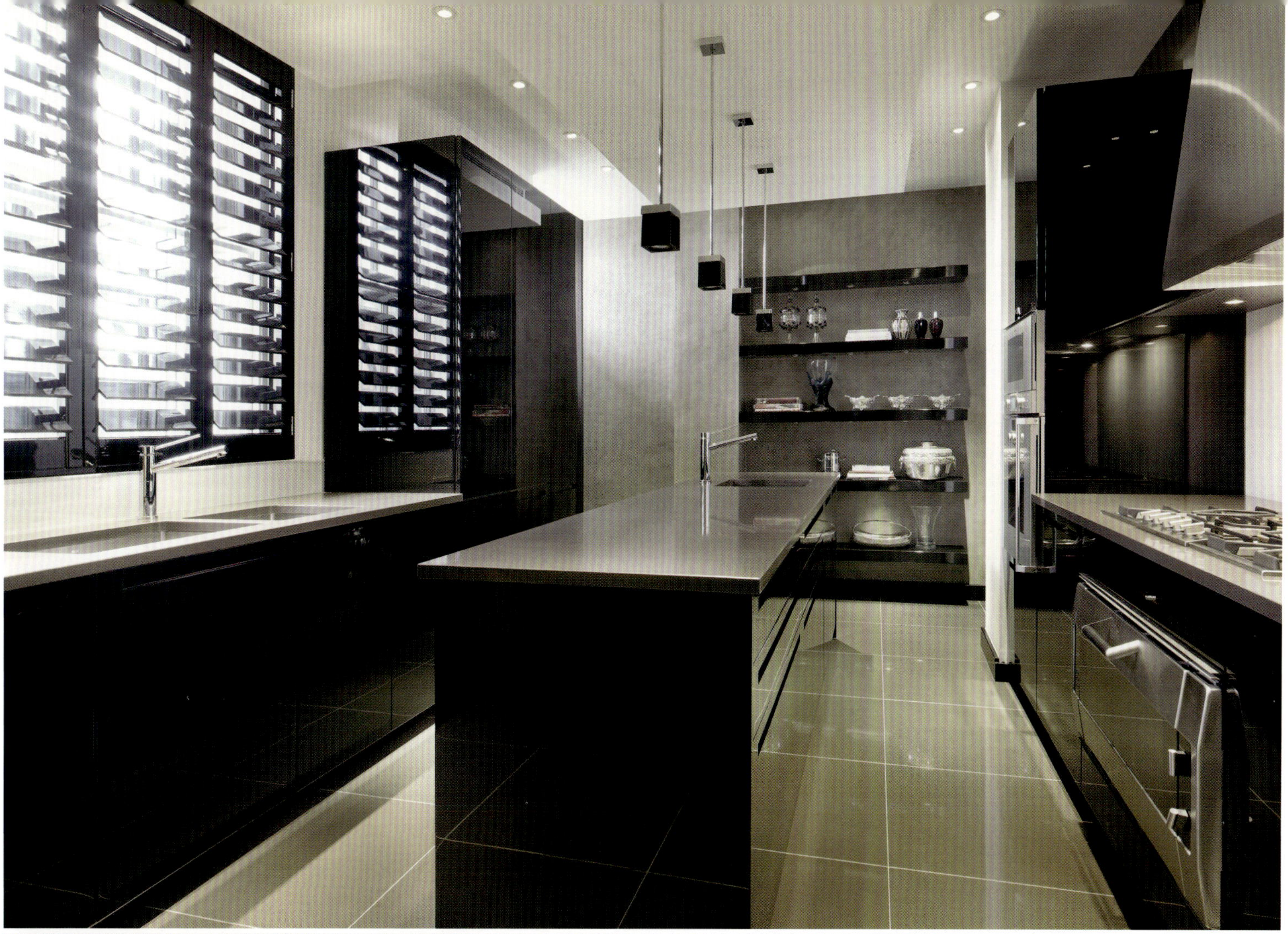

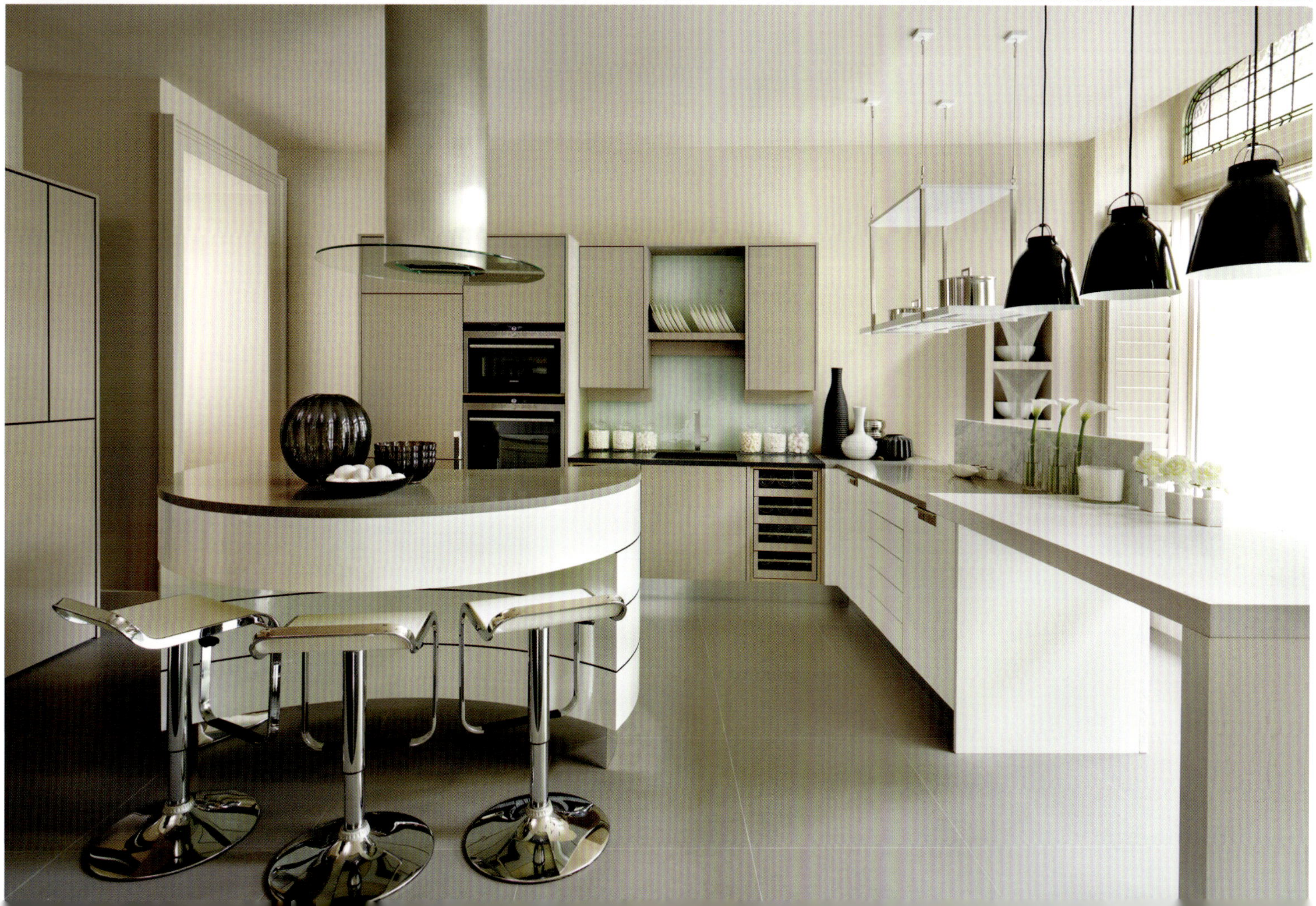

IN DETAIL
KITCHEN LAYOUT

00 You need a clear head when creating the perfect kitchen, so take your time at the planning stage and do your research thoroughly.

01 Built-in cupboards and appliances line three of the walls.

02 Twin island units impose symmetry on the space.

03 The rectangular shapes of the kitchen units and islands are balanced by the circular table and tub chairs.

04 Cooking and eating zones are signified by different-scaled lights.

05 Pairs of stools complement each island unit and ensure they double as breakfast bars, providing somewhere for friends and family to perch.

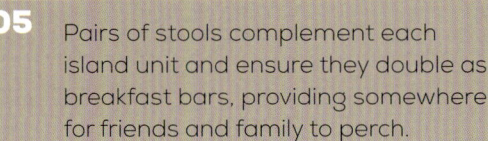

Above left and right Different vistas of the same Poggenpohl kitchen featured on page 202. As the plan (opposite) shows, the kitchen has been designed to allow for two island units, as well as cupboards and appliances that line the walls. In such a vast space, it is best to keep materials to the minimum – teak-style resin and quartz are the key materials here. The simplicity of the dining area has been challenged by the exuberantly over-scaled light by Fontana Arte, a deliberately playful juxtaposition against the row of under-scaled glass pendants.

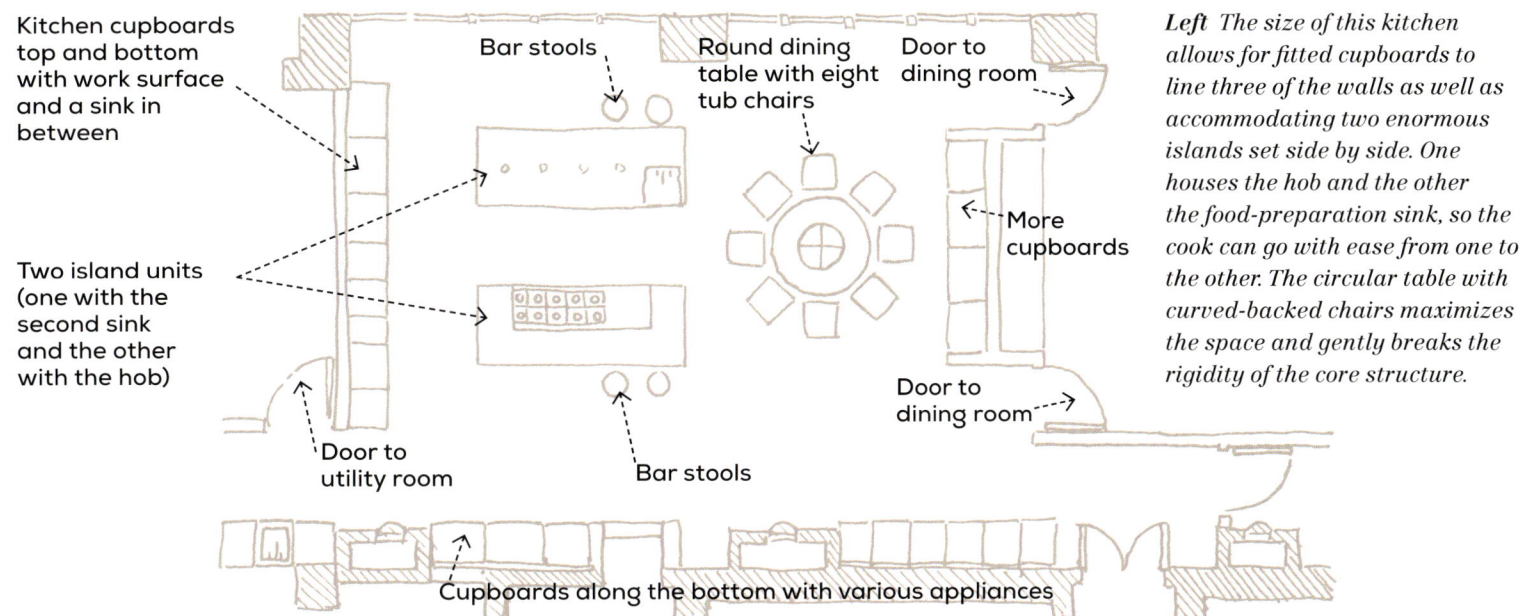

Left The size of this kitchen allows for fitted cupboards to line three of the walls as well as accommodating two enormous islands set side by side. One houses the hob and the other the food-preparation sink, so the cook can go with ease from one to the other. The circular table with curved-backed chairs maximizes the space and gently breaks the rigidity of the core structure.

Lighting

Designing lighting for a kitchen involves far more than ensuring you have good task light for cooking by. Because the kitchen is likely to be designed to incorporate a number of zones, it is possible to use lighting to demarcate these – soft in some parts and brighter in others. Don't just think about how much lighting you need at night; a kitchen has to be well lit and welcoming at all times, especially on dull winter days. Think, too, about lighting areas beyond. Rather than looking out at blackness at night, it can be wonderful to see a beautiful tree or shrub highlighted by a cleverly positioned spotlight.

The more circuits you have in a kitchen, the more versatility you have at your fingertips. Well-positioned spotlights are ideal as task lighting, with beams trained on sinks and chopping areas, for example. However, don't just rely on ceiling lights – a light source at low level, such as under the kitchen plinth, will create a soft wash of light on the walls and floors for added atmosphere. Under-cupboard lighting is always advisable, but top-lighting cupboards is also a boon, as it creates a wash of light across the ceiling. Add feature lighting, too, such as low pendants over a dining area.

As with all lighting (see pages 80–95), success lies in layering up different levels of light, from task, to mood, to statement. Dimmer switches are an easy way of giving lights even more controllability.

Left Low-level kickback lighting provides a soft wash of light on this timber floor – it can be dimmed for an even more intimate effect.

Right Warm-white LED lights are placed on top of the full-height units to bounce light off the ceiling and create a comfortable ambience. Recessed ceiling lights have been positioned to wash pools of light onto the front elevations of the doors. Under-unit lights provide task lighting, while the antique globe pendant lights and suspended rack of candles change the mood for evening entertaining.

Decoration and Detailing

If you are on a very tight budget, you might consider buying a budget kitchen. This can work well if you avoid faux finishes, such as mock oak or pine, and if you change the door furniture, which is often responsible for designs looking cheap. Spend money instead on a wonderful work surface, an eye-catching splashback and statement taps, as these are the design details that can really make a difference. Think glamour: just because the kitchen is ultimately a functional space does not mean you shouldn't create something drop-dead gorgeous.

So far as the floor is concerned, this has to be led by how much cooking and living actually go on here. In a high-usage family kitchen, maintenance is a key consideration (see page 206), but if this is a kitchen where you can allow yourself to push the boundaries visually, you can create textural interest through runners of stone in a poured-resin floor, for example, or by insetting natural matting into stained floorboards to define the dining area.

Walls should be kept as neutral as possible, so as to create the canvas against which kitchen cupboards and work surfaces are brought into focus. Ceilings, too, should go unnoticed, which is why you might opt for surface-mounted lights as opposed to recessed ones – the latter tend to show every fault in the ceiling plaster.

Kitchens should benefit from as much natural light as possible, so keep window treatments minimal. Shutters are excellent in houses where you want maximum privacy and quiet, but in a more secluded location – particularly if you have double-glazing – you might decide to have nothing at all at the windows.

When it comes to freestanding furniture, such as bar stools or kitchen tables, don't buy them all from one kitchen showroom, as the look will be very predictable. It is more fun to introduce a note of originality with vintage items or statement design pieces. Chairs are the sculpture of the room, so choose ones that are bold in form and interesting in texture.

Finally, as with other rooms in the house, choose art and accessories that add a layer of wit and personality. Kitchens should look clean and uncluttered, so a few well-chosen pieces will be enough to finish the look you have carried in your head since putting together that first concept board.

KELLY'S TOP PICKS FOR KITCHENS

- Units in textured wood or lacquer.
- Low-level pendant light suspended over a dining table.
- Retro bar stools at counters or islands for chatting.
- Feature splashbacks in marble, granite, glass, stone or concrete.
- Open display units.
- Customized drawer storage.
- State-of-the-art ventilation.
- Multi-layered lighting.
- Enormous fridge.
- Integrated dining – breakfast bar or table.

Opposite top left Even a simple bowl of eggs can become part of a textural still life, as with this glass bowl set against the textured wood of the kitchen units and honed grey granite of the worktop.

Opposite top right A simple row of three Arum lilies in tall glass vases complements the lines and textures of this beautifully considered kitchen, while also connecting the eye to the garden beyond.

Opposite bottom left Ribbed glassware provides an interesting focal point against the taupe and white of polished and lacquered surfaces.

Opposite bottom right Classic Wishbone chairs by Hans Wegner have an East-meets-West aesthetic.

A SENSE OF OCCASION
DINING ROOMS

Above An intimate dining space is delineated here by the glow of the pendant light over the dark wood table. Floating shelves filled with an interesting mix of books, vases and decorative objets add character.

Opposite The hand-blown glass bubbles of this spectacular light designed by Melogranoblu contribute to the theatrical ambience of this cool, contemporary dining room. The lacquered surface of the Baltus table is complemented by the matt leather upholstery of the Christian Liaigre Velin chairs.

Dedicated dining rooms have been undergoing a reappraisal in recent years. There was a time when they were considered rather redundant spaces, often used instead as home offices or playrooms. However, increasingly there has been a return to the idea of having a separate dining room, used mainly for entertaining, in addition to an informal dining zone linked to the kitchen. The latter is more likely to be used for family meals or relaxed supper parties, providing a contrast in mood and style to the formality of the dining room.

If you have room for both, it makes good sense. The joy of a dining room is that it becomes synonymous with special occasions, the place where friends and family gather for traditional Sunday lunches, celebrations, festivals and birthdays. It is more likely to be used in the evening, so you can be braver with moody colours, rich textures and bold artwork. By contrast, the kitchen-dining area is more of a daytime space and its design needs to be coherent with that of the entire room.

Whether you have room for both, or just one, remember that the dining room comes alive because of the people who gather there to laugh, talk and eat. You will achieve something wonderful if you keep this at the forefront of your mind and make comfort a priority. This applies not just to the chairs you choose – ones that prevent aching bottoms or backs – but also to the atmospheric lighting, the music you play, the food you serve and the care you take over dressing the table.

Key Considerations

First ask yourself one very basic but necessary question: how many people do you wish to fit around the table? Your answer will affect not only the size and shape of the table you choose, but also its design – in particular, where the legs are placed. You can buy a table that looks as though it will easily seat four people along one side, but if the legs are poorly positioned, you might find you can only fit three. If you are buying the table and chairs from different suppliers, you need to make sure that they are physically compatible. This applies to both the length and height of the table – few things are more uncomfortable than sitting at a table that is either too high or too low.

Remember, too, a table must be filled with people. There is no point buying one that seats twelve, just because you can, if you are more likely to entertain six. There are so many good extendable designs available, so buy one that can adapt to your needs.

The shape of table you choose will be determined by the shape of the room. Rectangular tables are a joy to dress, because they create an immediate grid reference within the room (see page 44). A rectangular or square table is the ideal canvas on which to place runners. If you are splashing out on a really wonderful dining table, consider commissioning one to order – perhaps wood with a bronze runner down the centre, or two contrasting shades of lacquer. Round tables have the advantage of allowing everyone to talk to everyone else, but they require more space than you might imagine, as people need to be able to move freely around the table when others are seated at it. Draw up a floor plan and use scaled furniture to ensure that you allow enough flow when deciding what size and shape of furniture to order (see pages 56–7).

In a dining zone – the continuation of an open-plan living and cooking space – you need a table and chairs that fit with the style and mood of the adjoining areas, while also imbuing it with its own character. The table is always the focal point, so choose one that will be the star of the room.

Left This view of the dining room shown on the previous spread gives the full impact of the light installation (which is, in fact, lit from above). Buttoned velvet chairs at each end of the lacquer-and-chrome table contrast in scale and texture with the beautifully conceived lines of the Christian Liaigre Velin dining chairs. The custom-made laminate grid above the console is by Kinon and is a visual continuation of the stone grid inset into the wood floor. The crystal floor light is by Mark Brazier-Jones.

Furniture

If the budget is tight, spend on the chairs rather than the table. This is because the table can always be covered and beautifully dressed, so arguably it could be made of simple plywood and nobody need know. The chairs, however, are like pieces of sculpture in an otherwise uncluttered room. Rather than buy a set that is all matching, consider shaking up the look by having, say, two over-scaled wing chairs at each end and three or four low tub chairs on each side. Introduce some wonderful fabrics through the upholstery, such as rich, dark velvets against lighter linens, or leather teamed with suede. Remember, too, that the backs of dining chairs are as important as the seats – you might introduce panels of contrasting colour or texture to make these a bold visual statement.

Storage is also important. The dining room is the natural place to keep tableware, glasses, linen and cutlery, so if possible allow space for a sideboard, buffet or dresser. These traditional pieces of furniture have now been rejuvenated in many interesting forms, materials

and textures, so you are sure to find one that suits your own style, whether it is a vintage find or an iconic piece of contemporary design. Make a note of what you want to keep here and carry the dimensions, such as those of extra-large platters, with you when you are out looking. Ask yourself whether you want to display tableware and glasses or keep them out of sight. Also, consider whether you need a serving area or a place to keep food warm. Think how you yourself like to entertain – as with other rooms, it is about what your own requirements are.

Above In a multi-zoned space, the dining area must both complement the adjacent kitchen and yet also create its own mood and character. Here the clean lines of the Boffi kitchen are echoed in the oak table, stained to match the timber floor. Low Wishbone chairs make a visual play against the boldly sculptural Tom Dixon wing chairs. Anchoring the scheme are the three pendant bell lights in lacquered steel.

Style

The dedicated dining room is a place where you can be brave in terms of decoration, because it is about giving guests a 'Wow!' moment. Since it is likely to be used more by night than by day, you can choose darker, more atmospheric tones and textures. Keep to a neutral palette, one in keeping with the rest of your home, but intensify colours to a degree. This is a space to dress with confidence.

Hard floors work well in dining rooms – and have practical advantages, too – but because the dining room is likely to lead off the hall, there should be some correlation between the two (see page 183). The best houses are those in which you move seamlessly from one area to the next, and the floor is the best way of ensuring that sense of continuity. The same applies to a dining zone adjoined to the kitchen – design the floor to lead the eye with ease from one area to the other. In rectangular-shaped rooms, runners on floors are particularly effective – such as two contrasting shades of wood or stone.

Curtains are likely to be drawn closed at night, so introduce glamour to the windows with layers of shimmering sheers, silks or taffeta. Allowing fabric to pool onto the floor adds to the feeling of luxury and extravagance.

IN DETAIL
DINING ROOM

00 Ask yourself when the dining room is most likely to be used and by whom, and is it a separate room or part of an open-plan layout?

01 Decide how many people you want to seat around the table and assess the room to determine which shape of table will work best.

02 Make sure that your chosen chairs are compatible with the table in terms of size, height, position of table legs and flow (see page 42).

03 Consider whether this is more of a night-time space or a daytime one and remember that the lighting must be as comfortable as the furniture.

04 Make sure you allow for sufficient storage appropriate for the items you wish to store.

05 Underpin the scheme with the grid – by using a fabric runner on the dining table, perhaps, or by incorporating one of contrasting material into its design.

06 Collect different sets of tableware, linen, cutlery and glasses that will enable you to create a variety of looks and moods.

Opposite top This elegantly controlled dining room has been designed to comfortably seat 18. The white-lacquered wood floor provides the framework for the taupe-lacquered table and unusual cross-legged chairs. Two large consoles are positioned against the windows, while a pair of ceramic pendant lights accentuate their symmetry. The white shutters, lacquered to match the floor, act as a subtle divide between this space and the next (see page 63 for the opposite view). The floor lamp at the far end of the room is Conversation Apparatus by Fadi Mansour.

Opposite below In a spacious dining room such as this, it is important to keep the layout of the furniture strong and simple. Attention is focused on the table itself by the grid of white-lacquered flooring against the natural timber. The two bold console tables emphasize the grid structure and provide a place for display. At one end of the room is a sideboard, with doors to the kitchen on either side, while shuttered divides at the other end open into the adjacent living room.

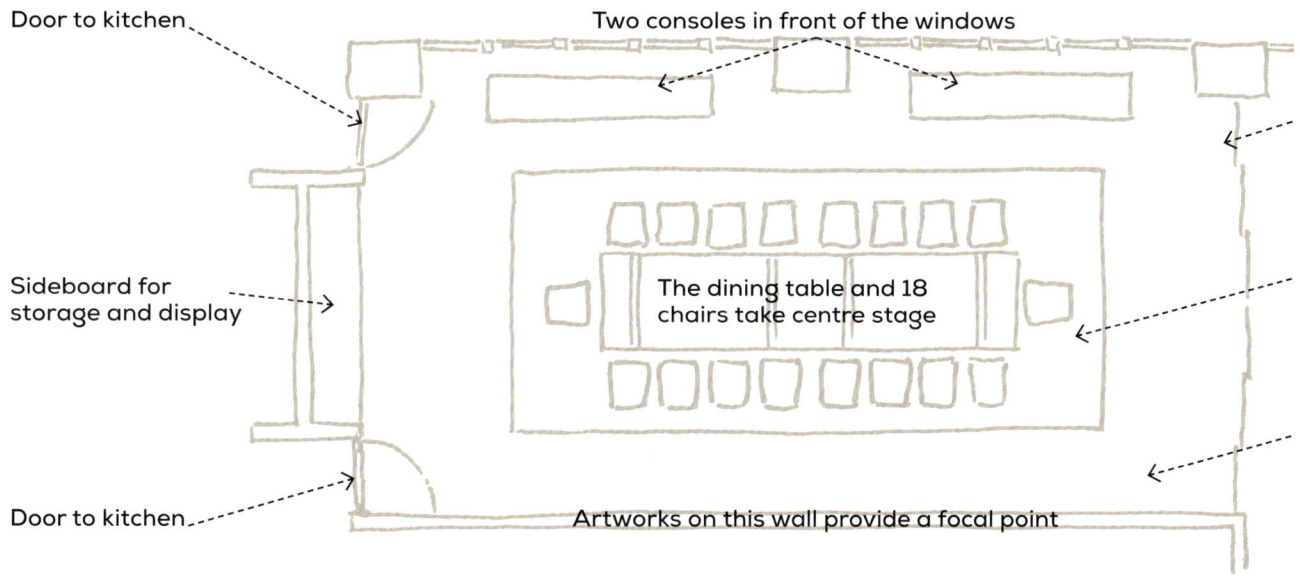

- Door to kitchen
- Two consoles in front of the windows
- Slatted screen doors which can be closed to divide the dining room from the living room
- Sideboard for storage and display
- The dining table and 18 chairs take centre stage
- The white-laquered floor frames the dining table within this large space
- The stained-wood floor creates a walkway around the table
- Door to kitchen
- Artworks on this wall provide a focal point

A SENSE OF OCCASION | 221

Lighting

Whether the space is formal or informal, well-considered lighting is key to the success of a dining room. Glittering crystal chandeliers, huge industrial pendants or other bold statement lights look particularly wonderful when hung low over the table, having the effect of drawing people together beneath them. However, if you want to have a low pendant light, bear in mind that you cannot also introduce tall candelabras, as the two will fight for space.

Candles are the natural accompaniment to dining, but as they cast very little actual light, you will need to boost their effect with indirect, subtly placed additional light sources. However, do not light your dining room so brightly that guests feel self-conscious and uncomfortable. If you have chosen a fabulous textured wall surface, make sure this is enhanced fully by wall washers or floor washers to add an additional layer of beauty.

Dining rooms are often the natural place to display collections and artwork, and these also require good lighting. If you are lighting paintings, photographs, *objets* or sculpture from above, use filters to distribute light evenly and reduce glare. If you want to highlight a small work of art, use a tight beam of light that really throws it into focus: this is particularly important in a room with a high ceiling.

Opposite top Gold metallic feature pendants cast soft pools of light onto this dining table, creating a dramatic interplay of light and shadow against the Kelly Hoppen flock wallpaper. Wall-mounted up-down lights wash indirect light up onto the ceiling, which is particularly effective when the lights are dimmed in the evening. The fire adds a further layer of mood lighting.

Opposite bottom left Multiples of three or four pendant lights hung over a table add theatre, but it is important that they are hung at a height where they do not obstruct the view of diners when seated.

Opposite bottom right Chainmail chandeliers by Ochre produce ambient light in a dining room, supported by additional layers of recessed lighting that wash light onto books and objets. The table lamps are dimmed for entertaining.

CGI: DINING ROOM LIGHTING

This CGI illustrates a design for a dining area, complete with lighting detail to show how the effects will work within the finished scheme. Trimless ceiling recessed lights have been positioned close to the window in order to wash arcs of light onto the curtains, accentuating the textures of fabric and flooring. The same lights have also been placed elsewhere in the room to highlight artwork. The bookcases are backlit with warm-white LED strips, which create a silhouette effect that enhances the displayed objects. Over the table are three distinctive crystal pendants by Ochre that demarcate the dining area and create a feeling of warmth and intimacy around the table. This is the benefit of CGI – not only does it give an accurate rendition of what the finished design will look like, but it also shows how specific lighting will enhance fabrics and furniture.

Accessories

While flowers, candles, art and collections of pleasing objects are all a boon to a dining room, adding to its atmosphere and personality, it is the table that really counts. You can transform the whole look of a room by what you put on the table. Consider, for example, what kind of mood gold plates denote, compared to black porcelain, compared to creamware. Think of your table as a perfect still life on which you can play with textures, colours and shapes. This applies as much to informal dining areas as to separate dining rooms.

The more choices of tableware, linen, glasses, cutlery and so forth you acquire, the better – nothing is duller than to lay the table in the same way over and over again. These items do not have to be expensive, so enjoy ringing the changes and creating looks for different occasions.

You might also have additional covers or runners made for your chairs, so that these, too, can be dressed according to the season or festival. If you keep to a neutral palette, you can jazz up the look of a room with bursts of bold colour, not on every chair but on a few – a little can go a long way in the right setting.

Opposite A simple row of creamy 'Norma Jean' roses is displayed in a variety of glass vases down the centre of this taupe-lacquered table.

Above A white wooden table with a freestanding mirrored runner creates the ideal setting for a sumptuous display of crystal and glassware. The distressed finish of the antique console, on which stands a collection of hand-blown vases, complements this perfectly. The artwork is by Ann Carrington.

KELLY'S TOP THREE WAYS OF DRESSING THE TABLE

01 Informal and Summer
White or cream ceramic tableware without chargers, clear wine glasses, pale green water glasses, white cotton cloth with a taupe linen runner and matching folded napkins, simple seasonal flowers in glass test-tube vases.

02 Formal and Winter
Taupe porcelain tableware on dark wood chargers, dark red wine glasses with clear crystal tumblers, no cloth but a taupe linen runner down the centre of the table and knotted linen napkins, moss balls shaped like miniature topiary.

03 Special Occasion
Heirloom china on silver platters, silver wine goblets and plum-coloured water glasses, grey damask cloth with a dark red silk runner and brightly coloured silk napkins folded on the plates, low troughs of dark red roses.

A SENSE OF OCCASION

PRIVATE MOMENTS
BEDROOMS

The bedroom is the last place you see when you go to sleep and the first place you see when you wake in the morning, so it has the biggest influence on your state of well-being of any room in the house. It is a place for deep relaxation, where peace and quiet are essential, but it is also where you dress, talk, read, make love and enjoy countless other activities. Everything within the bedroom should be designed to engender calm and comfort, from the way the bed is dressed and the furniture is arranged to the textures, colour palette and lighting.

Bedrooms are not just about what the eye sees, but also about how the room feels. They should be luxurious, sensual places, whether this is achieved through silk carpet underfoot or the velvet-edged linen that your fingers touch when you draw the curtains. While guest bedrooms should generally echo the design and decoration of the rest of the house, the master bedroom can be an exception. Being wholly private from the rooms shared with friends and family, it is a place where you can express your personality entirely. This really is a room that is all about you.

If you have space for a separate dressing room, then make the most of this advantage (see page 238). Bedrooms cluttered with shoes and clothes can never be the indulgent sanctuaries that they should be. Edit down what you keep here to the bare minimum, focusing on surrounding yourself with those items that really mean something to you and that make you happy every time you look at them.

Left A custom-made drawer and shelf in oak 'float' against the plaster wall of this pared-down bedroom. The lamp is a block of clear cast glass with a plain linen shade.
Opposite At the base of this bed is a concealed TV cabinet with metal Mondrian-inspired detailing. Specialist plaster runners on the wall at each side of the bed provide a backdrop for crystal lights, while under-lit floating bedside cabinets complete the feeling of luxury and opulence.

Key Considerations

The bed is naturally the focal point of the bedroom, so it should be placed as centrally as possible – the first thing you see when you walk in. It also has to be super-comfortable, so never skimp on its quality and design, or that of the bedlinen. Accord your guests the same privilege, so they leave your home feeling as though they have had the best sleep ever.

Headboard, bedcover and cushions should be designed together on one fabric board, as it is their cumulative effect that makes the impact, rather than their individual parts. Choose a bedcover fabric that looks and feels wonderful, perhaps a shimmering satin or a baby-soft cashmere, and then design a headboard that will complement or set this off beautifully, with runners in contrasting textures. Cushions should echo the bed as a whole, but may also bring in a new texture, such as wool, velvet or mother-of-pearl.

HEADBOARDS Even in a room dedicated to sanctuary and privacy, there should be a hint of drama – and the headboard is the ideal place to introduce an element of that. An over-scaled headboard – whether very tall or very wide – makes a bold design statement. It is also the perfect place on which to accentuate the grid, as well as providing a canvas on which to juxtapose contrasting materials and textures: leather, faux suede and linen are all versatile choices.

DRESSING THE BED When it comes to dressing the bed, introduce layers of sensuality with beautiful fabrics, such as cashmere, mohair, velvet, damask or the softest linens. Using one colour in varying tones, rather than different shades, never fails to look both elegant and luxurious. Stay with white, taupe or pale grey for bedlinen, either in linen, or in cotton with a high-quality thread count, and introduce a tonal colour on the headboard, bedcover and cushions.

Whether you prefer a duvet or blankets, have a bedcover made that covers the bed entirely, creating a neat and ordered look. Do not skimp on dimensions – a bedcover should 'pool' in swathes on all three sides.

To dress the bed properly, add rows of cushions. There are various combinations of sizes and shapes you can use, but a failsafe option is to have two square ones at the back (56 x 56cm/22 x 22in), two smaller squares in front of these (46 x 46cm/18 x 18in) and two rectangles at the front (46 x 23cm/18 x 9in). Cushions are the ideal place on which to introduce bands of contrasting textures – such as velvet on linen – further emphasizing the grid. You could also embellish them with buttons or trims (see also page 159).

Changing the bedspread and cushions is the quickest way to transform a bedroom from winter to summer, so do consider having separate sets made for each season. It is such a lift to the spirits to bring fresh, light, airy fabrics into a room when spring dawns, but also wonderfully comforting to add cosy layers of damasks and velvets when the days are darkening. The bed fabrics should be reflected in window treatments and furniture upholstery, so make these as seasonally versatile as possible, too.

Below A velvet, vertical-stitched padded headboard denotes comfort and luxury, complemented by patterned linen cushions with contrast stitching detail.

Opposite top Linen curtains, a linen-upholstered bedhead and a linen, buttoned bedspread create a soft, calm canvas. Brushed bronze pendant lights complement the abstract iron wall sculptures.

DRESSING THE BED

→ Choose sheets in white, taupe or silver-grey.

→ Decide on one quiet shade for the bedspread in a luxuriously tactile fabric.

→ Make sure the bedspread pools on the floor, rather than just touching it.

→ Have a choice of runners for the bed to reflect seasonal changes.

→ Scale up the size of the headboard so it makes a statement.

→ Upholster this in a fabric that echoes the rest of the room's scheme.

→ Buy a set of square pillows as well as rectangular ones.

→ Add two, four or six cushions in varying sizes, shapes and textures.

Right *Linens in various colours and weights are in perfect harmony with the smooth-finished plaster wall and crystal light.*

This page This unusual random-weave mirror from Christopher Guy makes a spectacular statement against the tranquil tones of a luxuriously layered bedroom. The faux-leather buttoned headboard has been extended to provide a backdrop for the floating shelves and drawer, on which stands a bronze lamp with a linen shade.

Opposite Mirrorball lights by Tom Dixon not only provide illumination but also bounce light around the room, as does the mirrored trunk that replaces a conventional bedside table. The runner on the wall is grey polished plaster.

Furniture

Don't clutter the bedroom with furniture, but do include a few pieces for practicality. Apart from wardrobes or chests-of-drawers for clothing (unless you have a separate dressing room), it is useful to have at least one occasional chair. This can be the ideal place to introduce vintage character or to experiment with bolder than usual upholstery choices.

You might also want a dressing table, either traditional or contemporary. A console table or a deep floating shelf fixed in front of a floor-to-ceiling runner of mirror creates an elegant alternative to the standard freestanding sort – just add some good task lighting and a stool.

Finally, think about whether you want a television in the bedroom and, if so, whether it will be concealed or on display. Audio-visual systems need to be planned from the very beginning, so try not to come to this decision too late in the day. Even if you do not watch TV in bed, the chances are you will want to listen to music or to the radio.

Style

In a space dedicated to relaxation, it makes sense to keep colours calm and neutral. However, bedrooms must be – literally – feel-good places, so when putting the design board together, concentrate on introducing fabrics and materials that are pleasing to the touch as well as the eye.

In bedrooms, most people like carpet wall-to-wall, or cosy rugs on wood – it is part of the sensual satisfaction of climbing out of bed and feeling softness and warmth underfoot. The most beautiful and tactile carpets are silk, lambswool or sheepskin, each of which injects warmth and luxury into a space. The floor is an ideal place on which to create runners of carpet or wood that emphasize the underlying grid structure of the room.

Window treatments should also combine sensuality with practicality. If you need a dark bedroom in order to sleep, blackout blinds are the answer. You can layer over these with beautiful sheers or floor-length curtains in glamorous silk, fine linen or velvet. Unless you need them to keep out draughts, don't have curtains interlined – then they can 'pool' to the floor, creating extravagant puddles of soft fabric. Shutters are a good choice in a room that you wish to keep relatively simple; they are practical, too, allowing you to let in as much light as you like. Generally, keep the walls plain – a specialist plaster finish behind the bedhead is enough to add a subtle and effective layer of interest.

Above left A Kelly Hoppen bed in white leather is the eye-catching centrepiece of this peaceful bedroom.
Above right In the same room, a cluster of iron-framed mirrors is functional and creates an art-style installation on the wall.

Top left and right *A custom-made wooden partition divides a bedroom from a dressing area. The bed is framed by two ceramic Jeremy Cole lights. The desk and chair are by Kelly Hoppen.*

Above *The rounded back of this B&B Italia sofa plays against the line of the floating ledge behind. The lacquered table is from the Kelly Hoppen range.*

Left *A white-lacquered cube table and steel light are effortlessly pure.*

Right *Bergère linen armchairs are complemented by a faux-leather stool. The fretwork-style side table has been hand-crafted in wood and painted glossy white. Floating shelves and a steel floor lamp complete the calm effect.*

IN DETAIL
MASTER BEDROOM

Design the master bedroom for your own comfort and needs, and remember that a bedroom is as much about touch as sight.

01 Buy the best bed and bedlinen that you can afford and create a fabric scheme for the bed that brings together a palette of beautiful textures for the bedcover, headboard and cushions.

02 Echo these fabrics in the window treatments and upholstery. Here linen walls are complemented by a leather headboard, a bedspread of textured linen and velvet cushions, both with linen runners.

03 Remember the importance of the grid in terms of design, whether it is reinforced by the banding on a cushion or a runner on the headboard or floor.

04 Choose a material for the floor that is warm and comforting underfoot.

05 Ensure that lighting provides versatile layers of task, mood and star pieces.

06 Do not clutter the bedroom with too many objects, but introduce a few that really mean something to you.

07 If possible, remove clothes and shoes to a separate dressing area.

08 Add flowers, candles and room fragrance that are very much 'you'.

Opposite top and above Linen-lined walls and a silk-viscose carpet cocoon the master-bedroom suite of this yacht in warmth and comfort. The faux-crocodile bed base and headboard add glamour, while the timber runner on the floor and up the wall underpins the grid structure of the design. The mirror conceals a television.

Opposite below In the same room, a lid on the custom-built ledge lifts up to reveal a hidden mirror and dressing-table storage.

Right The plan of the above bedroom shows how hidden space behind the headboard has been utilized to provide a compact bathroom to one side and a dressing room to the other.

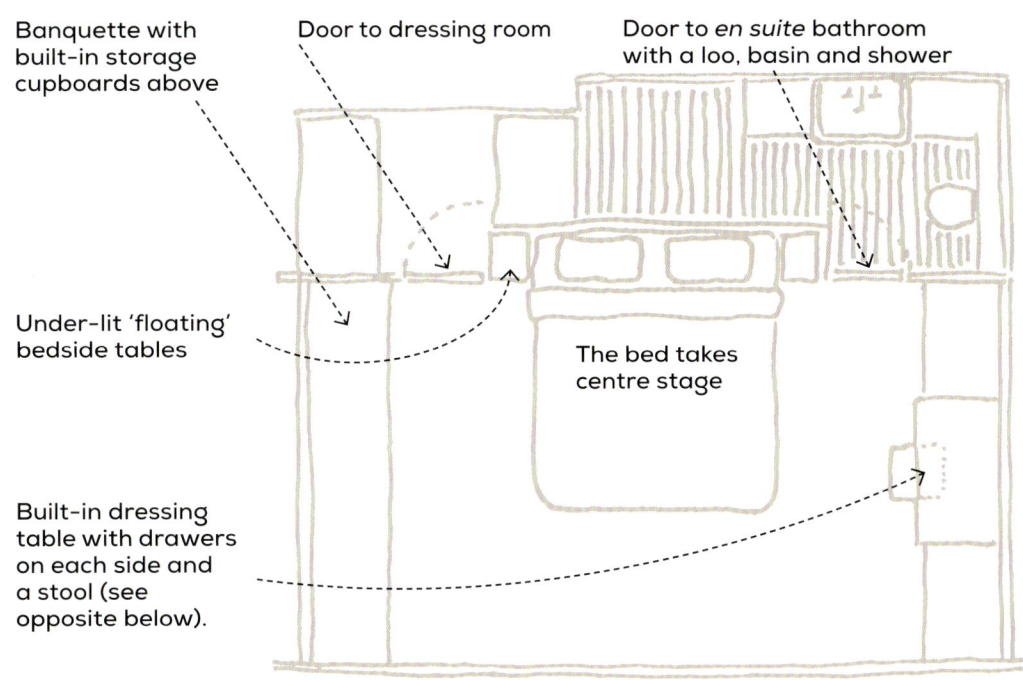

Banquette with built-in storage cupboards above

Door to dressing room

Door to *en suite* bathroom with a loo, basin and shower

Under-lit 'floating' bedside tables

The bed takes centre stage

Built-in dressing table with drawers on each side and a stool (see opposite below).

Lighting

Good bedroom lighting is essential in order to create a calming and soothing mood. It needs to be planned at the earliest stage, so you can see whether you need additional circuits, power sockets or light sources. Ideally, allow for three or four circuits. At the very least, fit a dimmer switch to the main light. Remember that you need to allow for more lighting in winter than in summer, so the more flexibility, the better.

As with other rooms, it is a question of allowing for a minimum of three layers of light: task, mood and star pieces. Do not position a light in the middle of the room, but plan where it should be according to the layout of the bed and other furniture. If you have a dressing-table area, for example, you will need to light this properly in order to apply make-up. Direct lights are never comfortable to the eyes or flattering, so it is better to position either downlighters or uplighters to face the wall, so that indirect light is bounced back into the room.

Most people position lamps on each side of the bed, but for a more striking effect, hang two low pendant lamps instead. If you want to read in bed, the lights need to be adjustable so that you cast light onto the page, rather than reading in your own shadow. Alternatively, add some LED flexi-arm reading lights in addition to low-hung lamps.

Break the rules when it comes to lighting the bedroom. There is no reason why you cannot hang a beautiful chandelier almost to floor height in one corner of a room, for example, or float a cluster of crystal lights over the bed. Remember that the finishes and colours you choose for the bedroom will hugely influence how light behaves. Light will bounce around a bedroom designed with glossy and mirrored surfaces. Conversely, if the décor is mainly wood, plaster and dark finishes, light will be absorbed and so will result in a subdued glow.

In children's rooms (see page 240), night-lights are advisable for safety and comfort. It is also possible to incorporate the equivalent idea for adults, by fitting low-level floor lights that provide a soft glow when switched on to guide you towards the bathroom or down the stairs.

Above right A concealed LED light set into profile and fitted to the underside of the beds creates an unobtrusive night-light.

Opposite top left A glass ball chandelier with polished nickel shade adds glamour and theatre.

Opposite top right Under-lit bedside cabinets create a floating illusion, here complemented by the sparkling beauty of crystal wall lights.

Right and opposite bottom left Miniature reading lights that are individually controlled can be fitted onto bedheads.

Opposite bottom right Feature pendants hung at each side of the bed also free up space on bedside tables.

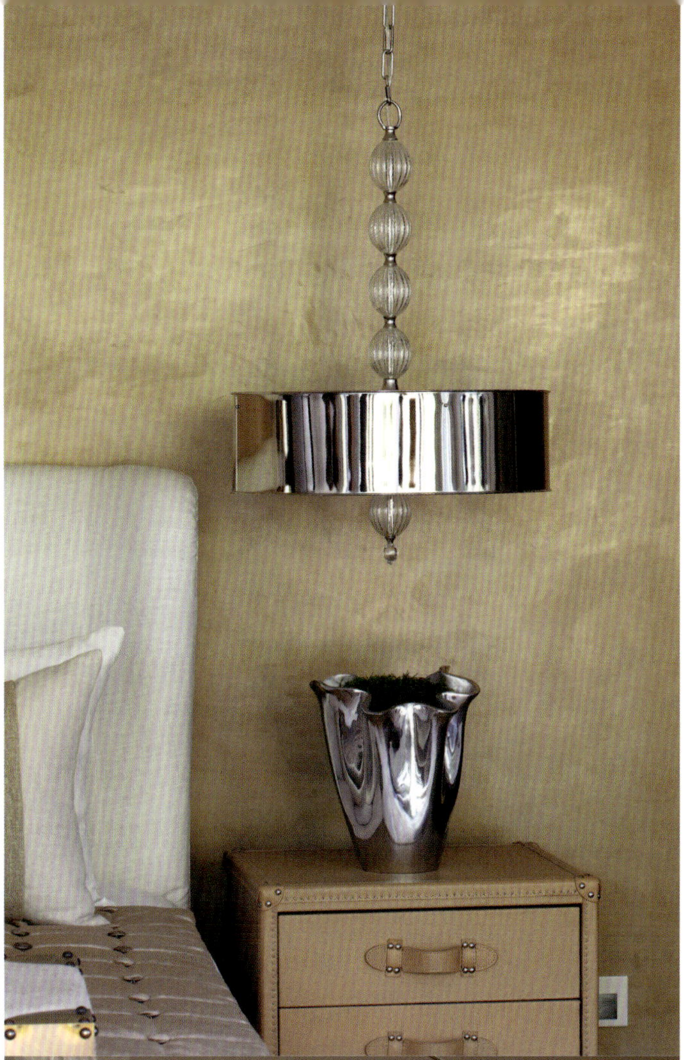
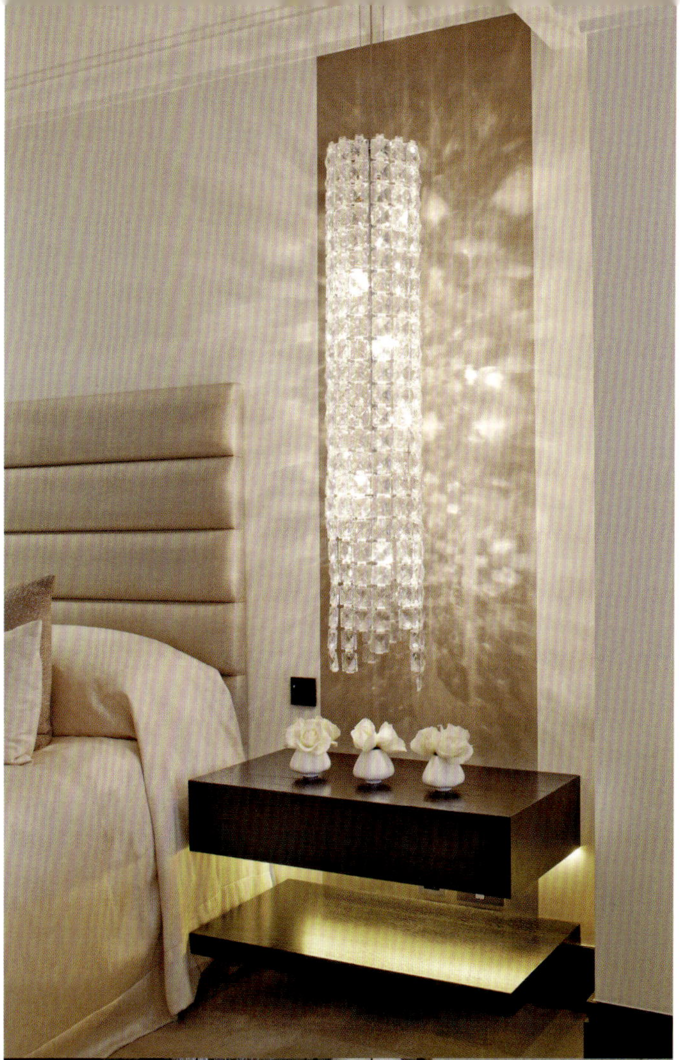
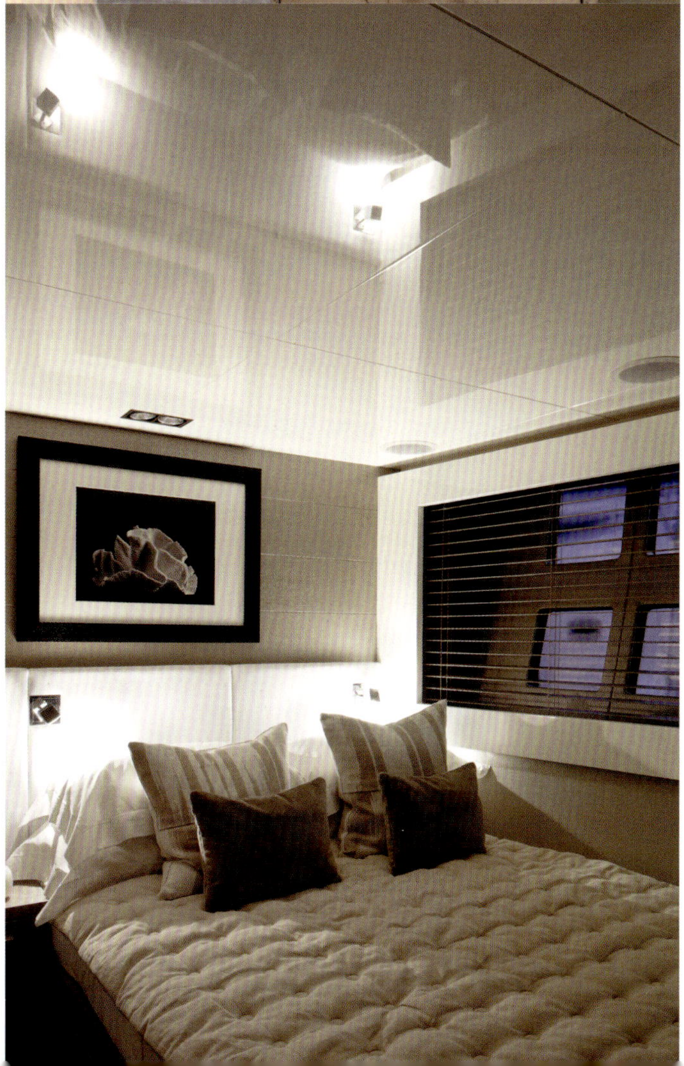
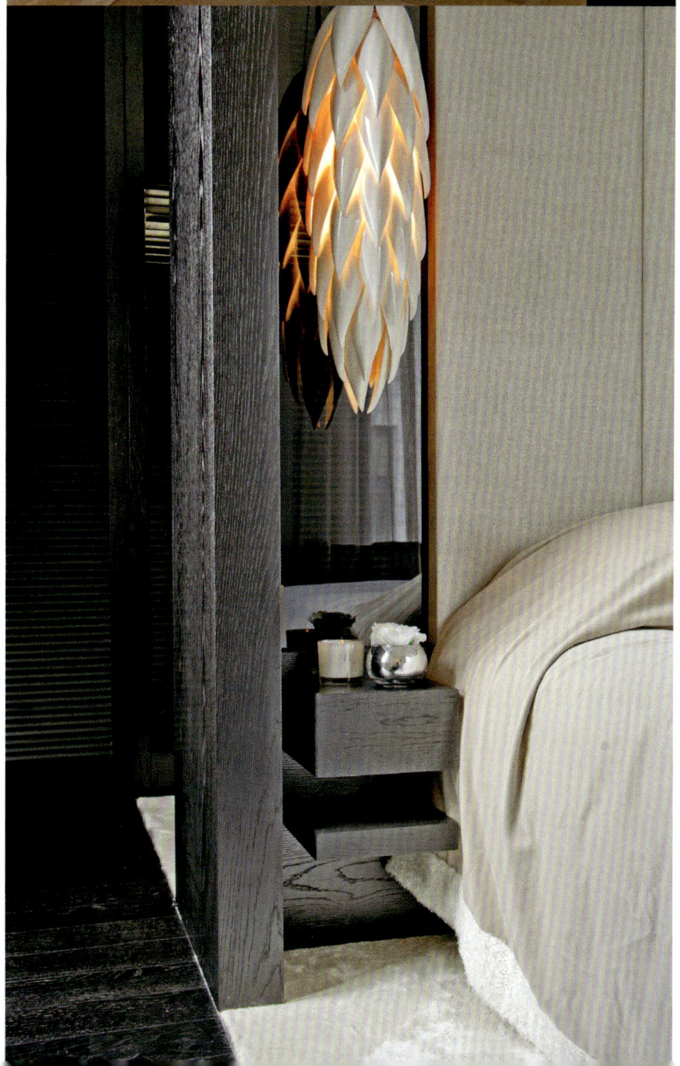

Dressing Rooms

If you are having joinery specially made for your dressing room, you need to design a system that is very personal to you. Think about what sort of clothes, shoes and bags you want to store here – and how many items you need to allow for. The storage you require for full-length evening dresses, for example, is quite different from that for jeans and T-shirts. Integrated lighting is useful, particularly if you favour black as a colour.

The wonderful thing about dressing rooms today is that – like kitchens – ready-made systems are a great deal more sophisticated than they used to be, so you really can design one that suits your wardrobe entirely, without breaking the budget. The secret then is to customize or change the doors, giving the impression that the whole room is bespoke.

Panelled doors give you the opportunity to juxtapose different textures, such as leather with wood or vellum with lacquer (see page 136). Incorporate detailing that adds interest, such as grooves in the door or particularly eye-catching door furniture in a contrasting material or sculptural design.

You may wish to include a dressing-table area in the dressing room (see page 232), but, if not, a low stool or ottoman and a full-length mirror are the only furniture you really need. The flooring, wall finishes and colour palette should all echo that of the master bedroom. Choose lighting that errs on the critical rather than the flattering – when getting dressed, you need to be confident that you really do know how you look before stepping outside.

Above far left Made in dark oyster-stained oak veneer with a combination of open and closed storage, this striking dressing area is full of visual interest. Additional drawers are concealed in the island unit and the velvet-cushioned bench.

Above centre In a dressing room where concealed storage is preferred, grooved timber doors add interest, particularly when they are illuminated, as they are here, both at floor and ceiling level. A pale bordered silk carpet leads the eye forwards, accentuating the room's length and depth.

Above right A different view of the dressing room shown above far left, with racks of shoe drawers and generous hanging space. Two large bronze mirrors are propped against the closets.

Children's Rooms

There is no reason why even very young children cannot help to design their own rooms. It is fun to sit down with them and create a mood board, working together to achieve the bedroom of their dreams. Children are so imaginative that you will learn a lot from listening to their ideas, and they are more likely to take care of a space that they have helped to create.

As with other rooms, think about function – a child's bedroom is not only a place to sleep, but also somewhere to hang out with friends, do homework, carry out hobbies and simply relax. If you can keep playrooms separate from bedrooms, it makes sense, because one is about being asleep and the other is about being very much awake. A room that doubles as both needs to be very carefully zoned (see page 41) in terms of furniture, lighting and styling, so that it can switch its mood between the two with ease.

Children's rooms are a joy to design, because you can really push the boundaries with inventive and imaginative schemes. Try to avoid trends or brands that will date. Keep the base neutral – white walls and plain carpet – but then inject excitement and wit with accents of bold colour on fabrics, bedlinen, storage systems or furniture. In this way, you can ring the changes as a child grows without redecorating entirely from scratch each time. Also, children's toys tend to be so garish that it makes sense to keep the foundation of the room relatively calm and peaceful.

Key pieces of furniture include an armchair, a desk and plenty of storage for clothes, toys and books. In addition, children's rooms should have some unexpected moments – perhaps a particularly fabulous lamp, a wonderful four-poster bed, a brightly upholstered iconic chair or a spectacular mural.

Left, top to bottom Hat-style hanging lights in white plastic are both practical and fun. White curtain fabric with raised dots, with a plain acqua linen border, adds a textural twist. The contrast ties on this lilac-coloured linen headboard add a feminine touch. A bright fuchsia Egg chair by Arne Jacobsen makes a bold statement.

Opposite top Soft shades of dusky pink and grey combine to create a mouth-wateringly pretty chill-out zone for a little girl.

Opposite bottom left The Paul Smith rug (from The Rug Company) has been custom-dyed to match this ultra-smart scheme conceived for a young boy. The lamps have also been sprayed to match the custom-made, deep-buttoned headboard. The stool is white plastic, as is the dog, used here as a child's seat, by Eero Aarnio for Magis.

Opposite bottom right A canopy bed in white lacquer is the star of this girly bedroom, decorated in fuchsia, raspberry and candy pinks. Coloured glass hearts are hung from the ceiling, to match the heart-shaped handles on the wardrobe doors and to reflect light around the room.

PRIVATE MOMENTS | 241

Left In this spacious playroom, a lightweight modular linen sofa with an array of brightly coloured cushions is complemented by ceramic side tables lacquered to match. The ties on the linen blinds echo the multi-coloured striped cushions below. The artwork in toning colours is by David Gerstein.

Below Green rubber flooring is soft, quiet and extremely practical in this super-chic playroom. A reinterpretation of the iconic Ball chair by Eero Aarnio has been upholstered in matching bright green linen. Child-scaled Louis XV chairs add a witty touch.

SPECIAL SANCTUARY
BATHROOMS

For most of us, the bathroom is the decompression zone between our busy, working lives and the calm we strive to achieve when at home. Whether it is an indulgent soak in a hot tub that you crave or the invigoration of a power shower, your bathroom is the punctuation point between day and evening, work and play, public and private.

The master bathroom is your sanctuary and the place where you can indulge yourself to the full. The Japanese understand this best with their tradition of cleansing thoroughly first and then enjoying the luxury of a long, deep soak. Warmth, comfort and highly efficient plumbing are musts, but so is engendering a relaxing, tranquil atmosphere. When you walk into your bathroom at the end of a tiring day, you should feel the cares slip from your shoulders.

It is likely, however, that you will also be designing bathrooms for other people in your house – children, teenagers and guests, for example. Bear in mind that they, too, need to feel cared for and cosseted in this most private of spaces. The bathroom must achieve perfect harmony between reality and fantasy, practicality and aspiration.

Left The white Thassos stone wall has been inlaid with a runner of pebbles bound in Riverstone resin, echoed in the same effect on the floor. The basin unit is lacquered in white gloss, providing a textural contrast to the matt of the oak panelled door.

Opposite Carrara marble panels line the walls and floor of this spectacular bathroom. The centrepiece is the white, sharply geometric bath with its contrasting dark panel, set against the marble tap unit.

Key Considerations

As a rule, it is best not to relocate bathrooms for the simple reason that the soil pipe and drains determine where the loo can go. If you do want to site a bathroom in another room, then you first have to find out whether it is practical to run the soil pipe to it.

There is no reason, however, why you cannot reconfigure the layout of an existing bathroom. Most can be hugely improved by placing the bath at centre stage, making it the focal point (as the bed is within the bedroom). It is the bath – and not the loo – that should be the first thing you see when you walk into the room.

While it is lovely to have a bathroom flooded with natural light, many *en suites* do not have that benefit, so the artificial lighting needs to be planned with even greater care to compensate for this. See whether there are ways of 'borrowing' light from the adjacent bedroom or dressing room. For example, rather than building solid walls between the two, explore ways of dividing the spaces with sand-blasted glass screens, plantation shutters or Japanese-style shoji panels.

Bathrooms are best designed around the idea of the grid (see page 44), which can be emphasized by runners in contrasting textures on the floor, walls and work surfaces. In many ways, the bathroom is one of the easiest rooms to design and decorate if you bear this principle in mind.

Opposite top left The oak-veneered, custom-built vanity unit, with a white Corian basin, is complemented by taupe stone inlaid into the cream stone floor.
Opposite top right The organic contours of this unusual freestanding basin are echoed in the coral and sand within the adjacent cylindrical vase. Simple wall-mounted taps keep attention focused on the sculptural star piece.
Opposite bottom left The restrained tones of stone-panelled walls and floor are the ideal backdrop to a bath of monastic simplicity. The taps are mounted into a matching stone unit.
Opposite bottom right The wrap-around design of this shower column and head denotes luxury and elegance in a marble-clad bathroom.
Left This bespoke stone sink has a sculptural quality. The timber runner on the stone floor is continued in mirror of the same width up the wall.

Style

When it comes to deciding on the look of your bathroom, first produce a concept board. Collect together images of bathrooms you like, pages from catalogues and magazines, examples of surface finishes and other decorative materials. You might choose to seek the advice of a designer in a dedicated bathroom showroom, but if you have a good plumber, you can probably tackle the bathroom on your own. Bathrooms are not as complicated as kitchens, because there are usually fewer options so far as layout is concerned. Neither do they involve complicated storage and work-surface solutions.

What sets the tone of the bathroom is the sanitaryware, so choose a style and design that you like but that are not too fashion orientated. Bathrooms are expensive to change – with lots of building upheaval – so you want to install ones that will still look good in five years' time. It is for this reason that white rarely fades from favour. Never mix finishes – if you opt for chrome in one bathroom, keep to chrome throughout. While it would be odd to choose different items from different ranges, you can make one exception with the bath. This is the star of the show, so you may want to allocate a major part of the budget to buying one with real impact and then choosing the rest of the sanitaryware from a less costly, but complementary, range.

If you are refurbishing bathrooms throughout the house, do not choose very different sanitaryware styles for each one, as the effect will be confusing. The only exceptions might be the master *en suite*, where you will probably want an extra-luxurious feel, and the guest cloakroom, where you could create something adventurous and witty (see page 256).

Be led by functionality more than looks. Some basins can appear very sculptural, but it will be maddening if they 'pool' water instead of draining properly. If you choose a heavy bath, ensure the floor joists will be able to withstand the weight once it is filled. Use floor plans (see page 56) to check not only that the sanitaryware will fit the bathroom, but also that it can be carried up the stairs and into position.

Taps are the sculpture of sanitaryware – a pivotal decorative detail – and come in a huge variety of finishes, styles and mountings. Most baths and basins come with a choice of recommended taps, but if you want to go to a different supplier, then be aware that not all taps fit all sanitaryware fittings. Don't be tempted to buy antique ones, as they can present all sorts of technical problems due to internal deterioration; it is better to buy reproduction versions, if that is the look you want. Wall-mounted and floor-mounted designs need to be fitted in advance of wall and floor surfaces, so allow for this when planning the building schedule.

QUESTIONNAIRE: FUNCTIONALITY

A bathroom must meet the needs of its users, be it you, your family or your guests. Ask yourself some key questions:

→ Who mainly uses this bathroom?

→ Do you want a shower or a bath, or both?

→ Can the shower be over the bath or must it be freestanding?

→ If freestanding, will it be a walk-in shower, a tray or a wet room? (Seek professional advice if you want a wet room, as fully tanking a room is complicated.)

→ Will the bath taps be wall- or floor-mounted or integrated into the sanitaryware?

→ Is the bath to stand on the floor, be raised on a platform or be sunken? (If sunken, seek structural advice.)

→ Will the basin be in a vanity unit or freestanding?

→ Would you like a bidet?

→ Do you want a concealed cistern for the loo and, if so, will you incorporate niches for display into the design?

→ Is safety a consideration in terms of flooring choice? (Answer yes if you have young children.)

→ Where is the best position for the towel rails?

→ Do you require any extras, such as a massage slab, sauna or steam room?

Once you have answered these fundamental questions, allocate plenty of time to visit bathroom showrooms and get a feel for all the options that are available to you. Also, begin to consider your lighting options, underfloor heating, ventilation and whether you want to incorporate an AV system.

Above and far right Two more views of the wrap-around shower seen on page 246. The dark stone inlay in the cream stone floor creates a powerful energy in a compact space, taking the eye from the bath to the floating basin, and establishing symmetry between the shuttered window and the panel of mirror opposite.

Right A dark lava-stone runner in a white stone floor leads the eye down the length of the bathroom to the recessed shuttered windows. The chic monochromatic colour scheme is accentuated by the bespoke vanity unit, floating shelves and carved door.

IN DETAIL
BATHROOM LAYOUT
Create something both functional and phenomenal.

01 Grids give structure to small rooms, such as bathrooms. Here the stone floor has been inlaid with glass mosaic.

02 Stone is not just practical in a bathroom – it can be a dramatic ingredient, as with this boldly figured Calcutta marble.

03 Try to budget for some star pieces, such as this wrap-around shower column and head.

04 Freestanding baths are akin to pieces of functional sculpture, as with this egg-shaped design.

05 Taps can be mounted separately from sanitaryware. This graceful floorstanding version is a Kelly Hoppen design.

06 Make sure you have plenty of storage. Black oak floating shelves are the ideal solution for this bathroom.

Layout

Study a floor plan of the room and use scaled cut-out paper models of the bath, loo, vanity unit and shower tray to decide on the best layout (see page 56). Try to visualize what you will see as you come through the door. If it helps, go into the room and mark out the position of key items with masking tape on the floor and walls. Be practical: a towel rail needs to be close to the bath and the shower, not on the other side of the room.

Think, too, about how certain plumbing choices will affect the look and layout. If you want to have a concealed cistern on the loo, for example, this will mean building out the wall to accommodate it, which in turn creates the perfect opportunity to incorporate niches or shelving for display.

Once you have decided on the layout, you can return to the idea of runners (see page 44), either as horizontal or vertical features. These should be used to emphasize the placement of key features, such as the bath and basin. An effective design is to run a contrasting material across the floor from the door and up the wall, framing the basin or bath and leading the eye forwards. As a rule, the smaller the space, the bolder the grid should be. Don't overcomplicate the design: grids are usually best achieved by laying stone into wood or vice versa, or by using two contrasting stones.

Opposite and above The striking marble-clad walls and floor form a canvas for a compact bathroom with very pure lines. The all-glass shower enclosure does not detract from the stone's visual impact. A complementary runner of glass mosaic leads the eye across the room from the basin to the bath.

Right The floor plan shows how the grid cuts centrally across the room, marking out the optimum positions for the bath, basin and shower, and creating balance within the layout.

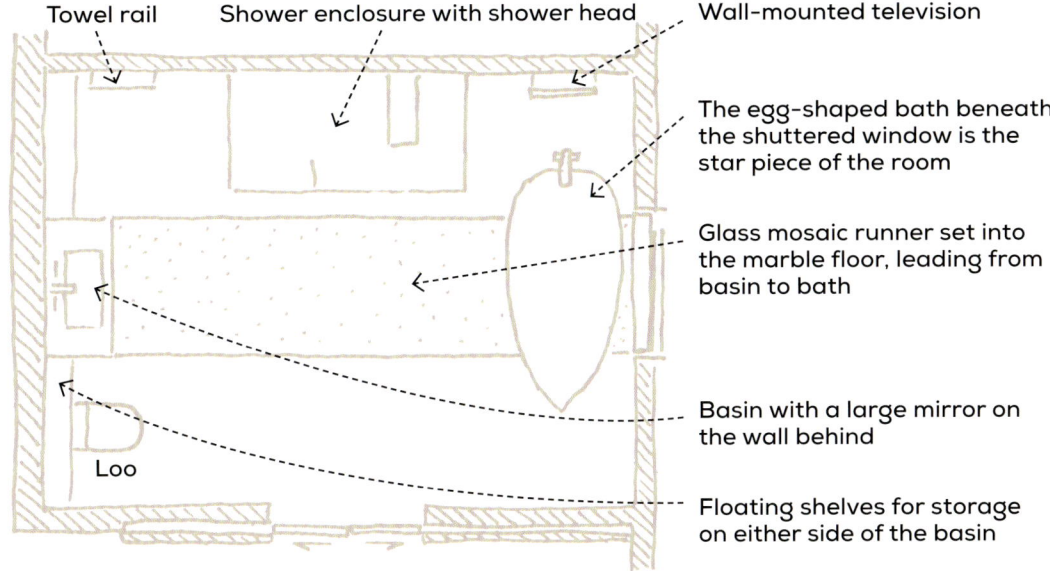

- Towel rail
- Shower enclosure with shower head
- Wall-mounted television
- The egg-shaped bath beneath the shuttered window is the star piece of the room
- Glass mosaic runner set into the marble floor, leading from basin to bath
- Basin with a large mirror on the wall behind
- Floating shelves for storage on either side of the basin
- Loo

SPECIAL SANCTUARY

Lighting

The secret of good bathroom lighting is to combine layers of task lighting with layers of mood lighting (see pages 80–95). Ideally, you should have at least three circuits in the bathroom: one for task lighting, one for ambient lighting and one for general light. The addition of a pre-set system will allow you to have five or six changes of light and atmosphere at the push of a button – ideal when you need a bathroom that is bright and refreshing in the morning, but dim and soothing in the evening.

When it comes to planning the task lighting, think about what you actually do in the bathroom – such as applying make-up, styling your hair or shaving – and design the lighting accordingly. Try to avoid placing recessed lights directly over your head when you are standing in front of the mirror, as this tends to cast shadows over your face (and is also very ageing). It is better to have light facing you, integrated, perhaps, on two vertical fittings on each side of the mirror in 'Hollywood' style (vanity units often incorporate this idea). It is best to avoid fluorescent bulbs, which are rarely flattering – tiny wall-mounted spotlights are much kinder. A dense cluster of small starlight fittings integrated into the mirror will also provide good light, but make sure they are on a dimmer so that you can brighten or soften the light according to task and mood. For a truly flattering light, bounce halogen light up onto the ceiling above you, so that it washes down over your head, bleaching out any shadows.

Concealed low-level floor lighting is an excellent way of washing the floor with light, creating an ambient effect. Lighting the tops of cupboards is also an effective solution,

creating washes of light over the tops of walls and across the ceiling. It is all about creating balanced waves of light across the room, for a soft and sensual effect.

If you long for a feature light, such as a chandelier or a similar statement piece over the bath, don't despair of safety regulations. Hang one regardless, but do not have it wired. Instead, position spotlights above it to wash light through, so creating a glamorous, sparkling effect.

Opposite left The floating wall positioned behind the bathtub has been fitted with concealed warm LED strips that define the space and illuminate it beautifully. The floating wall appears to be framed by the light that washes over the surface of the wall behind.

Opposite right Low-level lighting washes the floor with pools of light, a particularly relaxing effect when the lights are dimmed. The niche is lit by a recessed light in the ceiling.

Above left The alcove lighting in these shelves creates an interesting display area. Low-level floor washers and concealed lights in the underside of the vanity unit add a further layer of light and mood to the task lighting above.

Above A concealed LED strip behind sand-blasted glass is both functional and attractive. Light bounces indirectly off the walls – a far more flattering effect than would be created by overhead recessed lights.

SPECIAL SANCTUARY | 253

Decoration and Detailing

It is possible to buy decent sanitaryware on a budget – keep to white and choose a design that is as low-key and classic as possible. To make it look more luxurious, spend extra on great taps – the sculpture within the room (see also page 248).

Stone flooring is a good choice for a bathroom, not least because it is the ideal companion to underfloor heating. Make sure you select flooring that will not be too slippery when wet, particularly if you have children (composites or rubber may be safer). If cost is an issue, you can make a small amount of fabulous stone go a long way. Instead of cladding walls entirely, just use it over the wet areas of the room and contrast it with something relatively inexpensive, such as ceramic tiles or tongue-and-groove cladding. Maintenance can be an issue in a room that gets so hot and steamy, so take advice on how to protect timbers and stones from staining.

If you have a bathroom with big windows, make the most of natural daylight by opting for window treatments that maximize light. Plantation shutters, textured glass, runners of linen or airy sheers may be ideal, but bear in mind that you may need additional blinds at night in order to guarantee privacy.

KELLY'S TOP EIGHT BATHROOM MATERIALS

1. MARBLE 2. SLATE
3. WOOD 4. GLASS
5. MIRROR 6. CONCRETE
7. TEXTURED PLASTER
8. STONE OF ALL SORTS

Avoid introducing too many different materials. Grids are best designed around a simple combination of two textures: wood and stone, two contrasting stones, or perhaps a resin with stone or wood. Milk glass, available in any colour you choose and less costly than stone, is also a good option. In a child's bathroom, you could combine wood and rubber, which are both safe and durable.

One material that is a must in the bathroom is mirror. Not only does it make a room appear bigger, but it also adds another layer of texture and glamour. Use it as the third core material of the room.

Good storage is essential, so make sure your design allows for plenty of cupboard, shelf and surface space. A freestanding bath might require a small table nearby to compensate for a lack of surrounding storage space. Remember to allow for the storage of small-scale items, such as cotton-wool balls or cotton buds, as well as for bulkier items, such as loo rolls. For a truly couture bathroom, work with a master joiner to create built-in cabinetry with a customized space for everything from toothpaste to towels.

Add character and interest with a few well-chosen pieces of furniture – a beautifully upholstered chair or day bed, for example, will act as a softer foil to all those hard surfaces. A well-placed collection of decorative objects adds a note of personality and wit. Flowers, books and scented candles should all be viewed as part of the decorating palette.

Opposite top left The timber runner on the floor continues up the block step and beyond the shower enclosure, onto the stone wall behind.

Opposite top centre A glass shelf wraps around the contours of this marble-and-stone bathroom. A collection of textured glass vessels makes an interesting display.

Opposite top right This shower cubicle is set into marble walls with runners of lava stone on the floor. Recessed lighting adds to the atmosphere.

Opposite centre An unusual square, wall-mounted towel rail is seamlessly streamlined.

Opposite bottom left The inverted L-shape of this washbasin and shelf unit is a witty juxtaposition against the sumptuous Carrara marble of the walls and floor. The runner of mirror introduces the grid, which is reinforced by the horizontal lines of the floating shelves.

Opposite bottom centre The block step and tap panel have the same purist lines as the bath itself.

Opposite bottom right A white stone runner on a black timber floor creates a bold grid against which the basin and shelf appear to float.

Guest Cloakrooms

The joy of the 'smallest room' is that it offers the chance to take a few risks and break some rules in design terms. While the rest of the house should be designed with flow in mind, in order to create a seamless transition from one space to the next, the guest loo can be a moment for unexpected drama and boldness. However, do not confuse this with being 'fun' or gimmicky. The effect must still be overwhelmingly fabulous.

For one thing, in a small space you can afford to use more luxurious materials. This might mean choosing a really amazing marble, a hand-crafted plaster finish, an antique mirror or a spectacular chandelier. Introduce grids and runners (see page 44), but scale them up so they really make an impact. Monochromatic finishes are particularly effective – this is the only room in the house where you could team a white loo with a black basin, for example. Consider your guests' comfort, too – mirrors must be well lit so that make-up and hair can be checked, towels must be abundantly stacked and you should install the largest basin the space will permit.

Below left A runner of stone set into the dark timber floor is picked up by the runner of mirror of the same width. Wall-mounted taps do not detract from the impact of the Corian basin.

Below centre A runner of mirror reflects the carved detailing of the door and storage unit behind. The dark tones of the black granite basin complement that of the wood and the specialist plaster walls. The taps have been mounted onto the mirror.

Below right The same cloakroom as seen below left, showing how a simple light brings out the textured finish of plastered walls. Dark glass vases with single hydrangea heads make a pleasing display.

Opposite A ceiling-mounted tap over a bespoke bowl-like stone basin is unexpected and inventive. The walls and floor are lined in glossy, taupe-coloured Italian stone, complemented by the collection of glass-and-nickel bottles.

DOWNTIME
EXERCISE AND LEISURE ROOMS

This page Golden-brown geometric plastered walls complement the gold of the mosaic tiles that form a central runner down the length of the pool. The glass section of ceiling at the far end allows light to enter the pool area, creating interesting plays of sunlight and shadow.

This page A wall of riven quartzite makes a spectacular statement wall at the far end of this mosaic-lined pool. The adjacent wall is a specialist plaster finish and the floor tiles are textured and slip-resistant. The spectacular chandelier of Perspex rods is, in fact, washed with light from concealed light sources above.

What could be more luxurious than your own indoor pool, hammam and sauna? Many people today are harnessing technical sophistication and engineering know-how to dig beneath their properties and install subterranean pools – often entire fitness suites – running the length of their garden. The challenge is keeping these spaces coherent with the rest of the house. Take inspiration from hotels and spa retreats, and think about how such areas should make you feel, as well as how you want them to look. These are rooms dedicated to making you feel refreshed, energized or deeply relaxed, so every sensory comfort must be considered, from air-conditioning to towels and scented candles. In many ways, pools are simple design concepts – a container filled with water – so in aesthetic terms it comes down to how you will clad, light and accessorize yours. Choose installers with care – there are many technical specifications required, so it is important to get these right from the start. Also, make sure the plant and controls are easily accessible for maintenance.

Pools and Spas

The first consideration is safety, particularly if you have children. It is advisable to have a security system, pin-pad protected, that prevents anyone from accessing the pool area without you being aware of it. You should also choose flooring materials with care.

The pool is the ideal place to play with texture, because the design is centred on the hard surfaces you choose for cladding the pool, floor and walls. There are so many varieties and colours of stones, slates, bricks and tiles available that you can design your pool area to create an atmosphere that is light and airy or dark and moody, according to the materials selected. It is essential to take specialist advice, as many stones will 'rust' when saturated with water – your supplier will not necessarily tell you this unless you specifically ask. Consider how easy the materials will be to maintain, as well. Ceramic tiles are the obvious choice for pool areas – practical, hard-wearing and available in a multitude of colours – but you need to ensure that the grouting will not look discoloured and dirty within months of installation.

Textural contrast is what makes a room come alive, so you might combine rough brick with smooth ceramic, dark slate with creamy marble, or glass tiles with limestone. Three hard surfaces should be enough to play with, as you will add interest through the additional layers of light and a few simple accessories, so don't overcomplicate your design. If you want to include something softer as a contrast to the hard surfaces, specialist plaster effects are the perfect foil to the earthiness of stone and brick. Pool rooms lend themselves very well to the idea of the grid, because most pools are rectangular, so you can accentuate their shape with runners of contrasting stone, for example. Be bold – these are large rooms that need a confident eye and vision.

Even in underground spaces, encourage natural light in through well-positioned skylights. These don't have to be central over the pool – they are just as effective when placed at one end or in slim rectangles running in line with one side. Designing layers of lighting is essential for creating mood and ensuring safety. The distance from the surface of the water to the ceiling is greater in a pool room than in a bathroom, so there is more flexibility in the type of light fittings allowed and you may be able to hang a fabulous design. An electrician will be able to advise on the IP (ingress protection) rating allowed, which rates the degree of protection against moisture.

Think about how to zone the pool area for comfort and efficiency. How many changing cubicles do you need? Do you want to include a steam room, sauna or massage room? Maybe you would like a seating area, with or without a television? Where you place each zone and how they flow from one to another is key to the overall success.

Every zone within a fitness suite must converse visually with the others. A small area, such as a steam room, is the perfect place in which to use a really bold marble, even if budget dictates it can only be on a feature wall. However, a secondary material must link to other areas within the suite. Any furnishings will need to be able to withstand heat and steam, so ask for advice. Finally, introduce some accessories to bring the pool area alive – anything with height and scale that will not appear lost in such a cavernous space.

Top The black mosaic walls and marble floor of this super-chic steam room have been cleverly lit to give depth and interest.
Above An over-sized white-lacquered mirror on smooth plastered walls reflects the soothing serenity of the massage room in this home spa. Nickel, Deco-inspired wall lights add to the ambience, as does a console table adorned with flowers, towels and candles.

Gyms

In order to design a gym that is perfect for you, first be honest about what you will actually do there and the equipment you need. Most people like to have a cross-trainer, a running machine and a floor mat, but you may also want space for Swiss-Ball work, a barre for ballet, a set of weights, a rowing machine and so on. When drawing up the floor plan, be practical about the size of room you have and what will fit in comfortably. You won't enjoy exercising if everything is too close together and you haven't left enough floor space for Pilates, yoga or stretching.

Ideally, one wall should be mirrored, so you can see exactly what you are doing and correct your posture if necessary. The floor must be super-practical, comfortable, quiet and durable, so rubber or wood are good choices, as they feel warm underfoot. If you are a dancer, you might need to install a sprung wood floor.

A gym is not supposed to be decorative, so keep it simple with white walls, a plain floor and elegant joinery. Comfortable lighting is a must – you don't want light shining in your eyes if you are doing mat work, so consider having floor-level light sources that shoot light upwards instead. Decorative pendant lights can also work well, but these should be positioned over a specific workout area, not centrally. Add a few individual touches, something to make the space personal to you, such as some wonderful wall-hung photographs. If you want to watch television while working out, make sure it is hung at a comfortable height. One thing that is essential for fitness is great music, but remember that your AV system must be wired in before construction work begins.

Left Glass partitions separate the gym from the other home spa areas. This is further delineated by the change of flooring, from honed brown stone to stained timber. Two large freestanding mirrors are the sole accessories needed.

Opposite In a home cinema, linen-upholstered chairs with plaid and striped grey wool cushions denote a mood of relaxation. Electric-blue velvet stools and faux-suede walls add to the ambience of tactility and comfort. Lighting is subtly layered to provide just the right amount of darkness.

Media Rooms

Many people now require a home cinema or dedicated media room, because the television has become an increasingly dominant feature of our lives. Love it or loathe it, the fact is that many families like to spend their downtime together, watching films, sport, period dramas or classic comedies. By dedicating one room to television, it is possible to free up areas within the house for other activities.

The joy of media rooms is that there is no need to conceal or camouflage the screen, as this is the star of the space. Remember, though, that bigger is not necessarily better – the size of the television must be proportionate to the size of the room itself, or it will not make comfortable viewing. Seek the advice of a professional AV company.

Seating is obviously key to the room's success and should be as comfortable as possible. Choose beautifully tactile upholstery, such as velvet or chenille, so you can enjoy snuggling down in front of a great film. Plenty of cosy throws should also be available – children, in particular, love cocooning themselves in blankets when enjoying a family night in front of the screen. You can either choose to lay out seating in short rows – like a miniature cinema – or install modular sofas, stools, day beds and chairs, which can be reconfigured with ease. Side tables for drinks and snacks are also essential. Low-level lighting is a must, as is air-conditioning (the equipment produces a lot of heat). Thick carpet minimizes noise, as do certain wall materials, such as panels of fabric or wood. Now just sit back and relax.

PROJECT MANAGEMENT

The process of interior design is not only about being creative – and passionate about making your home beautiful – it is also about being super-organized. You have to understand every aspect of the project, from how to read floor plans and elevations (see page 56) to how to run a team and make a budget stretch. When you are being your own interior designer, the buck stops with you.

The Basics
Of all the qualities you need to have as an interior designer, organization is key. Renovating a home is a huge undertaking that involves many people. It is said that moving house is one of the most stressful things in life, yet, in effect, that is what professional interior designers do for a living.

Room by Room
You must retain control of your project down to the tiniest details. It helps if you allocate a folder for every room you are designing and divide this into sub-sections: walls, floor, joinery, architectural details (such as fireplaces), furniture, lighting, soft furnishings, windows, accessories, artwork.

When specifying your choices for each section, be as detailed as possible, so that you can estimate costs accurately. Remember that a choice of finish can have a big implication on the total price.

Arrange site visits with all the specialists you are involving, such as curtain makers, carpet fitters, specialist plasterers and so forth. Do not rely on estimated prices based on plans and elevations – only a site survey will result in an accurate quotation.

The Schedule
Intensive home renovation is a complicated dance between different trades, such as joiners, electricians, plumbers, stone cutters, audio-visual (AV) specialists, lighting designers and so on. If you are the project manager, you have to understand the exact order in which certain jobs are done.

GOLDEN RULES OF PROJECT MANAGEMENT

→ Be methodical. Tackle budgets, schedules, lead times and on-site deadlines in a calm, composed and ordered way.

→ Make folders for every individual room you are tackling and file all paperwork accordingly – plans, estimates, bills and so forth.

→ Duplicate references to fittings and materials for your builder, so that you are both clear on exactly what to expect at the point of delivery.

→ Make time each day to catch up on emails and other correspondence relating to your project.

→ Make lists every day prioritizing what is to be done on the following day.

→ Design timelines clearly showing the schedule of work and what has to be ordered (and delivered) by when.

→ Keep a dedicated up-to-date address book with the emails and telephone numbers of every supplier, contractor and professional involved with the project.

→ Ask builders, plumbers and other contractors to keep you notified about planned holidays and other absences – and enter these on your timeline.

→ Do not make hasty decisions when dealing with the hundreds of questions that will be fired at you from all corners.

→ Be helpful, but not overly accommodating.

→ Remember that you cannot know everything or do everything. Seek help and advice before it becomes critical.

→ Keep a sense of humour.

Take the bathroom, for example. It is obvious that the plumbing has to go in before the sanitaryware is installed, but you will need the sanitaryware on site so that your stone specialists and/or tilers can make templates on the floors and walls before cutting stone and tiles to fit. In fact, the sanitaryware may be one of the last things to be installed, but is the first thing to choose because of its impact on the rest of the design.

As project manager, it is up to you to enter each additional phase of installation on the Schedule of Works the builder has provided, clearly showing when other specialist trades have been booked by you and when deliveries of fittings have been arranged. If you make an error with any of this, you will hold up progress, because you could have a situation where builders can do nothing on site until the next link in the chain is in place. Any delay will also cost you money in additional labour days needed.

Here is a simplified schedule showing the many stages that have to be thought through:

- Strip-out and clearing of the site.
- Making good any structural faults.
- Removal or erection of walls (if necessary).
- First Fix Building (structural changes, such as new door openings and reconfiguration of space).
- First Fix Electrical (new wiring) and plumbing (new pipework).
- Second Fix Building (such as plastering of walls over new electrics).
- First Fix Joinery (skirting boards, floors and so on).
- Second Fix Electrical (wiring of new lighting) and plumbing (installation of sanitaryware and so on).
- Second Fix Joinery (shelves, cupboards, wardrobes).
- Decoration.
- Installation of carpets, curtains, furniture and soft furnishings.
- Accessorizing and artwork.
- Specialist cleaning.

Unforeseen Problems

Problems often arise during renovations. These can be anything from furniture arriving late or damaged to the schedule being delayed by one specialist trade not turning up when they should.

Keep calm and try to deal with the problem as quickly, calmly and efficiently as you can. On the whole, if you have been methodical about budgets, deliveries, running your team and so on, the problem will be relatively minor. A contingency fund should be in place to help just in case something requires additional money in order for it to be sorted out quickly.

Managing the Budget

One of the first things you have to determine is the amount of money you can afford to spend on the work you want to do. It is essential that you are honest about how much you can afford. The worst-case scenario is that work has to be halted midway because you can no longer afford to go on with the project.

Changing your mind after the event is the single, most expensive mistake you can make, so stay focused and take every decision after careful consideration. All too often budgets do over-run. While it makes sense to allow for a contingency fund of around 20 per cent, any increase greater than this should be avoidable by careful planning.

Don't make impulse buys for your home. That is the equivalent of popping out for a pint of milk and coming back with a pair of designer shoes. Everything must be accounted for on the spreadsheet.

Hidden Costs

The budget you have will not all be spent on furnishings, fittings and general home improvements. In fact, probably only around half of it can be spent on the things you would like.

A budget has to allow for:
- VAT (if applicable) on all costs.
- Professional fees (architect, surveyor, lighting consultant and so forth).
- Specialist fees, such as carpet fitters, tilers and stone cutters.
- A builder quoting a Provisional Sum on an estimate as opposed to the actual amount – usually this will be the lowest possible cost in terms of labour and materials, as opposed to the actual sum.
- Delivery costs.
- Additional services, such as the framing and hanging of pictures, Scotchgarding and specialist cleaning.
- A contingency sum for unexpected price increases and such like – 20 per cent is sensible.

How To Make a Budget Stretch

If you have done your sums and are now feeling depressed at the lack of money available, don't panic.

First of all, look to see whether there are any obvious areas that could be rethought.

The core works – bathrooms, kitchens, lighting, flooring, plumbing – are the expensive ones. Look for savings there. For example, moving bathrooms is costly, particularly because it involves installing new pipework and moving soil pipes. Perhaps you could revamp existing ones instead? Kitchens are also expensive – can you replace cupboard doors rather than rip out entire carcasses? Floors are another huge cost – can you utilize existing ones rather than replacing them?

You must allow for the cost of furniture, fabrics, art and accessories from the first, because you don't want to live in an unfinished home. However, you could make a plan of phases in which to do up the house – it is better to carry out the work in stages and get the quality you want, rather than restricting yourself to the cheapest of everything.

BUDGETING SUMMARY

→ Be realistic and honest about the budget you have available.

→ Do not waste money by changing your mind halfway through.

→ Make allowances for all the hidden costs, including VAT and professional fees.

→ Include a 20 per cent contingency fund.

→ Avoid impulse buys.

→ Beware of Provisional Sums (PS) on quotations.

→ If money is tight, plan improvements as a series of phases.

→ Be as detailed and specific as possible when asking for quotations in order to get a true picture of the money needed.

Assembling and Managing the Team

If you are putting work out to tender, ask for estimates from three or four builders, so that you have realistic comparisons of cost and time frame. Give yourself plenty of time to find the right people. Word-of-mouth recommendations are always good. Ask to see completed projects and, if possible, speak to previous clients for feedback. Meet builders to talk about the work and try to choose someone whom you feel you can trust, is reliable and has the experience and leadership qualities to run a good team. Don't always opt for the cheapest quote – what is important is ensuring a good standard of work at a reasonable price.

If you are very anxious about a project completing on time, write a penalty clause into the contract you have with your builder, stating financial penalties for every week that it runs over.

Remember that communication is the key to success. It is up to you to take your design brief (see page 54) and make sure that it is understood by everyone on your team. Briefing people well is at the heart of successful project management. Remember that you will be juggling a lot of people over the time a project takes to complete.

Depending on the size of the project, your team may comprise many professionals and trades, among them: architect (see page 268), structural engineer (who offers specialist construction and technical expertise), landscape architect, lighting designer, audio-visual (AV) consultant, home-security consultant, bathroom designer, kitchen designer, builder, joiner, electrician, timber and stone cutters, plasterer (general), specialist painter, tiler, decorator, and carpet fitter.

One of the challenges of running a project is making sure that everyone involved communicates well with everyone else – through you – so that work is never delayed because of one person not turning up on a particular day.

TEAM MANAGEMENT

- Choose your team with care.
- Consider having a penalty clause written into the contract should the project over-run.
- Follow the Schedule of Works day by day.
- Visit the site daily.
- Do not agree hastily to on-the-spot changes while on site.
- Plan to the last detail when each part of the project has to be completed and by whom.
- Understand the order in which work takes place.
- Do not allow building work to be delayed by long delivery times.
- Agree who is to take responsibility for checking deliveries.
- Remember that communication is key – and that ultimately it is your responsibility.

SITE VISITS

→ Ask the builder to provide you with a Schedule of Works – this is a timeline that will estimate week by week which jobs will be completed. It includes even the most minor ones, such as fitting power points and door furniture.

→ Agree in advance who will be responsible for taking deliveries and carrying out a quality check to spot any damage.

→ Visit the site every day and at different times of the day (the builder will be on his or her toes if he/she does not know what time you are likely to arrive).

→ Check the schedule every day with the builder. If it is falling behind, find out why – is there anything you can do to get it back on track?

→ You can tell a lot about a building team's efficiency from the state of the site. Obviously a certain amount of dust and mess is inevitable, but there should be a sense of ordered chaos. The best sites are those that are tightly run, with everyone stopping for allocated tea breaks at certain times, for example.

→ When visiting a site, never agree to on-the-spot changes to the design brief without going away and considering them first. Every change is likely to carry a cost implication. If you do agree to a change, put this in writing – an email will do – confirming the change and the cost.

Living on Site

If it is your own home you are renovating, you may prefer to live on site while work is carried out, but this may be a false economy. The fact is your presence will slow down building work. For one thing, you will restrict the hours that the builders spend on site, because they will have to fit in around you. Secondly, a lot of time will be wasted as they try to clean up each day in order for you to cook, bathe, sleep and so on. Thirdly, they will need to make the site safe in terms of electrics and plumbing before leaving each day.

Discuss the time implications of living in or moving out with your builder. The reduction of labour costs might mean that you can afford to rent somewhere close by for a month or so while the majority of the building work takes place.

Snagging

The final check of a project is known as snagging. This is the time to pick up any small imperfections that will irritate you if they are not put right – paint dripped onto power sockets, for example, or a tap that drips. Most builders are happy to put snagging right within reason, but you can hit problems if they refuse (understandably) to take responsibility for faults that were not of their making – for example, clumsy delivery men. This is where your contingency fund can again be useful.

Involving an Architect

You might consider employing an architect if you undertake a design project that needs more specialist knowledge or skill than your builder can offer. This particularly applies if you need special planning consents to achieve your vision.

An architect is usually the Lead Consultant on a project, co-ordinating the other professional disciplines involved, as well as the building team.

An architect is of help if what you are planning to do falls outside of your own comfort zone. However good a builder you may have, they are unlikely to have the design knowledge needed to create a truly elegant solution to a given problem. An architect will bring a whole new layer of knowledge and ideas to a design.

You are buying into a level of expertise that begins with the seven-year training. You are dealing with a registered professional who is bound by a professional code of conduct, and you can be secure in the knowledge that your architect has insurance should something go seriously wrong. In addition, architects will advise on the most recent regulations and requirements relating to the energy efficiency of buildings, because they are required to keep fully up-to-date by their code of conduct.

He or she can also recommend builders and other trades. If you accept their recommendation, there is much less chance of disputes arising on site, because the architect will take responsibility for their choice of contractor and the builder will want further work via the architect. Ultimately, the architect is someone who can take away much of the stress of a project, because he or she has already undertaken hundreds of similar jobs.

Fees are usually negotiated in one of two ways: as a percentage of the total building cost or as a fixed fee. Percentage-based fees are most common in a project where there is a fair amount of construction taking place (and costs are not entirely fixed). Fixed fees are most common where the scope of work can be clearly defined from the outset. This will have more appeal if you want to keep a tight grip on your budget. Architects usually consider projects in terms of work stages, charging a given percentage (agreed in advance) as each stage is completed.

Word-of-mouth recommendations are a good place to begin when looking for a suitable architect. However, you should always ask to see examples of work – either in a portfolio or (better) the real thing. There is a strong argument to support the idea of finding one who is relatively local – this will make site visits cheaper and potentially more frequent. It also means that the architect has previous experience of dealing with the local planning department.

WORKING WITH AN ARCHITECT

Architects contribute a whole array of specialist knowledge and skills.

- → They act as Lead Consultants, liaising with other professional disciplines and building trades on a project.
- → They can negotiate with statutory bodies, such as local planning authorities.
- → They can offer more design solutions than a builder is likely to be able to do.
- → They are registered professionals with their own indemnity insurance and code of practice.
- → While employed by the client, their responsibility is to remain neutral in order to solve any disputes that may arise.

Address Book

ANTIQUES

Alfies Antique Market
www.alfiesantiques.com

Portobello Road Antiques Market
www.portobelloroad.co.uk
Every Saturday

Sunbury Antiques Market
www.kemptonantiques.com
Second and last Tuesday of every month

Talisman
www.talismanlondon.com
Furniture and accessories

ART & PHOTOGRAPHY

The Affordable Art Fair
www.affordableartfair.co.uk

David Gill Galleries
www.davidgillgalleries.com

Frieze Art Fair
www.friezeartfair.com

KH Wall Art
www.kellyhoppenretail.com

Michael Hoppen Gallery
www.michaelhoppengallery.com

Stephanie Hoppen Gallery
www.stephaniehoppen.com

BATHROOMS & KITCHENS

Antonio Lupi
www.antoniolupi.it

Apaiser
www.apaiser.com

Dornbracht
www.dornbracht.com

KH for Crosswater
www.kellyhoppenretail.com

KH for Smallbone of Devizes
www.smallbone.co.uk

Modulnova
www.modulnova.it

Rexa Design
www.rexadesign.it

Rifra
www.rifra.com

FABRICS

Abbott and Boyd
www.abbottandboyd.co.uk
Fabrics and wallpapers

Andrew Martin International
www.andrewmartin.co.uk
Specialist fabrics

A One Fabrics
+44 (0) 20 8740 7349
Silk velvets and fashion fabrics

Bennett Silks
www.bennett-silks.co.uk
Silk and satin fabrics

Casamance
www.casamance.com
Contemporary fabrics

The Cloth Shop
www.theclothshop.net
Furnishing fabrics

Colefax and Fowler
www.colefax.com
Fabrics and wallpapers

de Le Cuona
www.delecuona.co.uk
Linen fabrics

Donghia
www.donghia.com
Textured fabrics

Fox Linton
www.foxlinton.com
Sheer, silk and suede fabrics

JAB
www.jab.de
Furnishing fabrics

J Robert Scott
www.jrobertscott.com
Furnishing fabrics

Kravet
www.kravet.com
Contemporary furnishing fabrics

Pedroso E Osório
www.pedrosoeosorio.com
Sheers and linens

Rubelli
www.rubelli.com
Specialist fabrics

Sahco Hesslein
www.sahco.de
Linen and other fabrics

Westbury Textiles
www.westburytextiles.com
Linens and other fabrics

Zimmer + Rohde
www.zimmer-rohde.com
Sheer fabrics

FENG SHUI

Richard Ashworth
www.imperialfengshui.info

FIREPLACES

B+D Design
www.bd-designs.co.uk
Bespoke fireplace sculptures

CVO Fire Ltd
www.cvo.co.uk
Modern fireplace installations

FLOORS

Belvedere Projects
www.belvedere.it

Borderline Carpet Planning Service (Trade only)
www.borderlinecps.com
Natural carpets

Byrock
www.byrock.co.uk
Specialist stone flooring

Crucial Trading
www.crucial-trading.com
Natural flooring and carpets

Dalsouple
www.dalsouple.com
Rubber flooring

Limestone Gallery
www.limestonegallery.com

Livra
www.livra.co.uk
Specialist stone flooring

Rimo
www.rimodesigns.co.uk
Rugs and carpets

The Rug Compay
www.therugcompany.co.uk
Handmade rugs

Top Floor UK Ltd
www.topfloorrugs.com
Rugs and timber floors

FLOWERS & GARDEN DESIGN

Absolute Flowers and Home
www.absoluteflowersandhome.com
Flower displays to order

Columbia Road Flower Market
http://columbiaroad.info/
Every Sunday

John Carter Flowers
www.johncarterflowers.com
Flower displays to order

Scent Floral Design
+44 (0)20 8203 5458
Artificial flowers

Sophie Eden
+44 (0)7768 222 206
sophie.eden@me.com

FURNITURE

Andrew Martin International
www.andrewmartin.co.uk

Arteriors
www.arteriorshome.com

B&B Italia
www.bebitalia.it

Baltus
www.baltuscollection.com

Casamilano
www.casamilanohome.com

Christian Liaigre
www.christian-liaigre.fr

Christopher Guy
www.christopherguy.com
Contemporary and classic furniture

Eames Office
www.eamesoffice.com

European Design Centre
www.edclondon.com

Gervasoni
www.gervasoni1882.it

La Fibule
www.lafibule.fr

India Mahdavi
www.india-mahdavi.com

KH Furniture Collection
www.kellyhoppenretail.com

McCollinBryan
www.mccollinbryan.com

Meridiani
www.meridianisas.it

Minotti Italia
www.minottiitalia.it

Modénature
www.modenature.com

Promemoria
www.promemoria.com

Robert Kuo
www.robertkuo.com

Sé London
www.se-london.com

Tom Dixon
www.tomdixon.net

Vitra AG
www.vitra.com

GLASS & MIRRORS

Chelsea Glass Ltd
www.chelseaglass.co.uk

HOME ACCESSORIES

Asiatides
www.asiatides.com

Atelier Vierkant
www.alteliervierkant.be
Indoor and outdoor pots

Bosa (Trade only)
www.bosatrade.it

C Best Ltd
www.cbest.co.uk

Home Style App by Kelly Hoppen
www.itunes.com

LEATHER

Alma Leather
www.almahome.co.uk

Edelman Leather
www.edelmanleather.com

Moore and Giles
www.mooreandgilesinc.com

LIGHTING

CTO Lighting
www.ctolighting.co.uk

Flos
www.flos.com

Heathfield & Co
www.heathfield.co.uk

Jeremy Cole
www.jeremycole.net

Kevin Reilly Lighting
www.kevinreillylighting.com

Lutron EA Ltd
www.lutron.com/europe
Lighting systems

Mark Brazier-Jones
www.brazier-jones.com

Melogranoblu
www.melogranoblu.com

Moooi
www.moooi.com

Ochre
www.ochre.net

Porta Romana
www.portaromana.co.uk

Roll & Hill
www.rollandhill.com

Robert Clift Ltd
www.robertcliftlighting.co.uk
Lighting designer

Spina Design
www.spinadesign.co.uk

Stéphane Davidts
www.davidts.com

Studio Bel Vetro
www.studiobelvetro.com

Todhunter Earle Interiors
www.todhunterearle.com

VISUALIZER

Dowling Jones Design
www.dowlingjonesdesign.com

WALLS

Graham & Brown
www.grahambrown.com/uk
KH wallpaper and wall art

KH Paint
www.kellyhoppenretail.com

Polidori Barbera Design
www.polidori-barbera.com
Specialist plaster wall finishes

WINDOWS

A&H Brass
www.aandhbrass.co.uk
Ironmongery

Fabricant
www.fabricant.co.uk
Curtain poles and finials

Izé
www.ize.info
Ironmongery

Joseph Giles
www.josephgiles.com
Ironmongery

Kelly Hoppen Shutters
www.kellyhoppenshutters.com

McKinney & Co Ltd
www.mckinney.co.uk
Poles and finials

Mumford & Wood
www.mumfordwood.com

Shutterly Fabulous
www.shutterlyfabulous.co.uk
Kelly Hoppen shutter range

Silent Gliss Ltd
www.silentgliss.co.uk
Track systems and curtains

Xavier Lebée
www.xasmvierlebeecreation.com
Ironmongery

FEATURED ARCHITECTS

Kelly Hoppen Architecture
John Cameron
+44 (0)20 7471 3350
www.kellyhoppen.com

Point 3 Design
www.pointthree.co.uk
+44 (0)20 8944 8095

Richard Mitzman Architects LLP
+44(0)20 7722 8525
www.richardmitzman.com

Acknowledgements

Every effort has been made to trace copyright holders of artworks and designs. We apologize in advance for any unintentional omissions and would be pleased to insert the appropriate acknowledgement in any subsequent publication.

My heartfelt thanks to all my wonderful clients who have allowed me back into their homes to photograph the results we worked so hard to achieve – without them this book would not have been possible. A huge thank you also to my amazing interior design team, who execute every job with such talent, intelligence and love. Special thanks to John, Tania, Lucy, Emma, Lee, Huei-Ju, Adam, Alex, Ines, Sineerat, Aruna, Priscilla, Hemma, Rhys, Thomas, Peng, Michael and Dustin for being so passionate about your work – you are my backbone.

Jacqui Small, thank you for everything – with every book, our relationship strengthens. To Helen Chislett, my huge gratitude for expressing my creative vision through such beautiful words with ease and understanding.

Mel Yates, thank you for the empathy you show when photographing my work. You have made our collaboration such a joy. Thank you to Lawrence Morton for your patience, calmness and boundless creative energy. And to Zia Mattocks for editing the book with such peerless professionalism – a particular asset for a dyslexic like me!

Rob Clift, a double thanks: not only do your lighting schemes enhance my work so beautifully, but you have also been so generous in sharing your knowledge and passion for the subject within these pages. Thanks to Hayley Newstead of Absolute Flowers for her glorious arrangements. To my visualist, Gregg Stone, my thanks for your hard work and unlimited creativity. Special thanks to both Doreen Scott and Thomson Schultz for making my soft furnishings with such care and attention to detail. Thanks also to everyone not mentioned here with whom my studio and I work to create such truly exceptional homes. Finally, my gratitude to the companies and individuals listed opposite, who form the backbone of my 'little black book'.

Credits

Artwork Credits

pp21, 77, 106 (bottom left) and 142–3 Zaha Hadid, Shelf 'Dune 01', 2007, Editions David Gill, London; pp25, 35, 45, 47, 50, 52, 53, 96, 114, 134, 194, 195, 214, 236, 237 and 256 all black-and-white photography by Simon Brown; p38 (right) paintings of paint tubes on canvas, both *Untitled*, by Arman; pp21, 38, 42, 81, 106–7 and 193 red and blue violin sculptures, both *Untitled*, by Arman; pp43, 63, 76 (far left) *Cor de Chasse* and (left) sliced trumpet cast in bronze, *Untitled* sculpture, by Arman; pp43, 63 and 76 golden violin in Plexiglas and bronze violin on marble stand, both *Untitled*, by Arman; pp43 and 63 (left) Jeppe Hein, *Triple Mirror Cut* (180 x 100cm), 2012, Courtesy Johann Konig, Berlin, 303 Gallery, New York, and Galleri Nicolai Wallner, Copenhagen; pp43, 63 and 76 photo-souvenir, Daniel Buren, *Made in USA*, zinc, travail situé, 2012. Détail © DB-ADAGP, Paris, Mel Yates; p54 Charles-Arthur Bourgeois, *La Danseuse Egyptienne*; p55 Dante Gabriel Rosetti, *Portrait of May Morris*; pp65, 79 and 97 George Romney, *Portrait of the Vernon Children*; p72 Amanda Brisbane, *Frozen Water*; p107 *Over and Over*, 2012 © Idris Khan/Courtesy Idris Khan and Victoria Miro, London; p110 *Kate in the Doorway*, 2005, © Mary McCartney, Courtesy of the Michael Hoppen Gallery; p121 Allan Forsyth, *Nightmare Decreases*; p135 (top right) gold and silver sculptures, both titled *Accumulation*, bottom pieces, both titled *Waiting to Exhale*, by Arman; p163 (left) Alf Lohr (www.alflohr.net), *Untitled* painting; pp163 and 166 *Lauren Bacall*, 1945, Scotty Welbourne, Courtesy of the John Kobal Foundation; p165 (top left) *MG Girl*, Simone d'Aillencourt for Elle, Paris, 1957, © George Dambier, Courtesy of the Michael Hoppen Gallery; p166 (right) *James Dean on the set of Rebel without a Cause*, 1955, © 1978 Sid Avery/mptvimages; p225 Ann Carrington, *Pearly Crown Jewels of England*; pp238–9 (centre) Ralph Brown, *La Fanciulla*; p242 David Gerstein, *A Couple of Strokes*.

Additional Design Credits

pp25, 35, 45, 46, 47, 50, 51, 52, 53, 85 (top left and bottom right), 102, 110–11 (centre), 114, 142 (far left), 155, 166 (top right), 170 (bottom), 171 (bottom right and top left), 178 (centre), 201 (left), 214, 222 (bottom left), 223, 233 (top), 237 (bottom right), 255 (bottom right) and 256 (bottom left and right), designed by Kelly Hoppen with Yoo, Russia.

pp26, 27, 28, 29, 30, 31, 32, 33, 74, 86 (far left), 87 (top right), 89 (centre), 91 (right), 92 (top), 98, 99, 101 (top and far left bottom), 116, 117 (top left and bottom right), 118, 119, 120, 121 (bottom left, centre and right), 124 (far left), 127, 130, 136, 137 (top row third from left, middle row third and fourth from left), 140, 149, 173, 178 (top), 184, 186, 187, 199 (far left second from top), 201 (right), 210, 211, 226, 229 (top), 231, 233 (bottom left), 237 (top left), 245, 246 (top right, bottom left and right) 249 (top and bottom right), 250, 251, 254 (bottom left), 258, 259, 261 (bottom), 262 and 263, designed by Kelly Hoppen for Regal Homes, flowers by Sophie Eden.

pp134 (bottom left), 172 (bottom left), 196 (centre), 204, 205, 207 (bottom), 213 (top left, top right and bottom left), designed by Kelly Hoppen for Smallbone of Devizes.

pp132 and 193 (top), Lounge chair and ottoman by Charles and Ray Eames, featured courtesy of Eames office (eamesoffice.com)/Vitra AG.

Fabric shown on endpapers: Elitis, Abbott and Boyd.

Additional Photography Credits

pp109, 111 (left), 121 (top), 163, 165 (top and bottom left), 166 (bottom left and right) and 225, photographed by Christophe Ichou (www.c-ichou.com).

pp46 (bottom left), 85 (top left), 114 (bottom), 142 (top centre), 167, 170 (top right), 171 (top left), 172 (bottom right), 196 (bottom left), 201 (left) and 214, photographed by Pavel Jovik.

pp40, 48–9, 85 (bottom left), 96 (left), 147, 165 (top right), 189, 193 (bottom left and right), 195 (bottom), 222 (bottom right), 232 (left and right) and 253 (top left), photographed by Nang Fung Developments.

pp25, 52, 84 (bottom left), 85 (bottom right), 102, 135 (top left), 155 (left), 170 (bottom), 171 (bottom right), 222 (bottom left), 237 (bottom right), 252 (left), 256 (left), photographed by German Sheyn.

p222 (top), photographed by Mark Whitfield (www.markwhitfieldphotography.com).

pp107, 108, 111, 112, 115, 150 and 151, photographed by A C Cooper (www.accooper.com).